God, Politics and the Future

SIS

Also by David E. Jenkins and published by SCM Press
The Glory of Man (The 1966 Bampton Lectures)
The Contradiction of Christianity
What is Man?
God, Miracle and the Church of England

David E. Jenkins
Bishop of Durham

God, Politics and the Future

SCM PRESS LTD

British Library Cataloguing in Publication Data

Jenkins, David E. (David Edward), 1925–
God, politics and the future.
1.Politics. Role of religion
I. Title
291.1'77

ISBN 0–334–02020–4

First published 1988
by SCM Press Ltd
26–30 Tottenham Road, London N1 4BZ

Printed in Great Britain by
Richard Clay Ltd, Bungay, Suffolk

Contents

Preface: The Way In

All the pieces in this book proceed from one simple and fundamental conviction. We must face the issue of God – that is,
the issue of what sort of reality, resource and glory 'he' ('she',
'it') is. What difference is made for us by the positive and
promising mystery which/who is at the heart of all things and is
greater than all things? Or, if there is no such mystery, then the
issue of the absence of God must be faced. We must not
promote lesser issues, lesser interpretations, lesser dogmatisms
and lesser ideologies into the role, status and function of a
'God for us' (whichever limited and partial 'we' we are). That
way lies idolatry, tyranny, persecution, the manipulations of
power and the excesses of consumption which will make life
more and more miserable for more and more of us before, in all
probability, they destroy us as a self-indulgent race on a small
but violated planet.

The 'we' who are under compulsion to face the issue of God
includes everyone without exception because the issue links
together the responsibility, prospect and destiny of each
and every individual and the survival, future and flourishing of every local community within that community of
communities which is the one global community. 'The one

global community' is no mere manner of speaking but a factual and descriptive phrase. We need look no further than the currently popular 'market philosophy' to see the truth of this. Markets are global, the computerized financial services industry and the credit systems are global, multi-national companies are global. In a grimly parallel way, weapons are global, therefore so is the community which seeks peace by preparing for war. Whether there are other more positive and more future-orientated aspects of our global community and our one world is a literally vital question which is of direct importance to every individual now alive or yet to be born. We all therefore have an interest in discovering what are the resources available for living with the one 'we' which we human beings now perforce, obviously and urgently, are.

The compulsion to face the issue of God is bound together with this pressure of being one human 'we' by a number of strands of argument and experience. For me, the central and most clearly compelling strand is what I glimpse, and what I believe to be revealed, of the glory and persistence and suffering creativity of God. This strand is also the Ariadne's thread which leads consistently onwards through the mazes, the muddles and the total darknesses, as well as through the mysteries, illuminations and celebrations, of actual human living in the world. These glimpses and these understandings of revelation have come to me, and do come to me, as a committed and, as I believe, called member of a Christian church, nurtured by the patterns of the Bible, stimulated by the living possibilities of the deposits of tradition and supported by worship and prayer which is as essentially communal as it is intimately personal. This is why the pieces in this book (all 'occasional' – given as sermons or addresses or lectures) are all a mixture of observation, explorations and arguments about some troubling and/or exciting aspects of our lives in the world joined together with references or broader argumentation drawn from the Bible and Christian tradition. Sometimes, no doubt, the mixture approaches to being, or actually is, a muddle. But to me that is an absolutely inevitable risk to take. I believe that God took and takes similar and much more profound risks in creation and underlines and expresses this risktaking in his incarnate identification with us as the man Jesus. I have tried to explore this aspect of things more in my previous collection of pieces on practical theology – *God, Miracle and the Church of England* – as well as in my earlier *Contradiction of Christianity*. Now I am concerned with the application of this faith, with discovering the differences which it makes, suggests or promises when we plunge into the questions, challenges and opportunities that our world, our society and our longings and fears thrust upon us.

This is where we come to the other strands of argument and experience which should act to persuade us that we must face the issue of God – or the issue of the absence of God. One such strand is the repeated failures in the practising of religion. Anyone who, like myself, continues to be compelled to believe in God, to seek God, and to respond to God, must surely be deeply troubled by the endemic ungodliness and inhumanity of so much of organized religion and of expressed religion. Churches, for example, whether at the level of their organized hierarchies, synods and committees or at the local level of their congregations, seem to be largely occupied with their own maintenance, manipulations and needs. Churches, therefore, tend to look like institutions preoccupied with providing packages of spiritual comfort for the private consumption of their active adherents while indulging in defensive battles against those realities of the world which seem to threaten their faith, combined with intensive battles among themselves about what to anyone but themselves would be either secondary or even pseudo-problems. The preoccupation of the church is, in practice, the church and not visibly either God or his world, which is a contradiction in terms. Further, church history contains far too many instances of intolerance, cruelty and power-mongering.

But this is not just a problem of the churches. They are not the only institutions whose behaviour, both as institutions and as expressed in their adherents, tends to become narrowly self-centred and frequently to betray the purposes for which the institutions exist. Similar behaviour is typical of all those institutions which emerge in human society to promote human survival and flourishing and to pursue goals related to human prosperity and well-being. Politics can become games of power and ideologies for politicians, only remotely related to the actual pressures of the survival and flourishing of the greatest number of those over whom they exercise rule. Professions become more profitable to their practitioners than of realistic service to their clients or to the community at large. Hospital complexes or industrial complexes can impose large system demands which make it more and more difficult to relate them to care in the community or products which the community really wants or can actually sustain. And so on.

Thus, as the churches so manifestly and so frequently fail to be godly in human saving and promoting ways and fall short of being human in ways which realistically relate godliness to most people's ordinariness, they represent, in a particularly acute and indeed scandalous way, the problem of all our institutions. Human institutions which grow up in response to various needs, necessities, insights, possibilities and even revelations in order to promote human betterment regularly become sources of human distortion, dis-service and even potential destruction. What resources are available to us to rescue us from our institutions, to renew us in and through our institutions and to enable us to pursue humane (and, it may be, godly) lives through our institutions, despite our institutions or apart from our institutions? This, again, is the question of

God, in its positive or negative form. Is there 'more' and how do we get in touch with and respond to whatever there is? In particular, and in the perspective from which all the pieces in this book arise, all convinced believers in God must surely find one of the sharpest pressures towards deeper and more urgent exploration into God arising from all those ways in which God-talkers and God-claimers contradict and contravene the very God we believe we are talking about. Can God rescue us from the contradiction of God? A glimpse of a positive answer to that question might be the most realistic and down-to-earth hope we could possibly have.

Hope is something which gets discussed, directly or indirectly, a good deal in the ten pieces which follow. It is the main theme of the first ('The Cost of Hope') and the last two ('Prospects for Peace' and 'How Green is our Future?'). This is surely very understandable, for one of the strands of argument and experience which affects us all and is woven into the issue of God is that of the threats to our survival. We have come very close to using up what might be called the 'margins of error' available for our human living on our planet, earth. Nuclear weapons, ecological erosions, resource consumption, increasing gaps between rich and poor and the heightening of social tensions because of divisions and exclusions do not leave us much room for manoeuvring by hit-and-miss blunders into a survivable and sustainable future. Are we simply near the end of our tether, with evolution on the verge of allowing us to extinguish ourselves (both with a bang and a good deal of residual whimpering)? Or can we together and responsibly use our immense powers of innovation, control, intercommunication and productivity to draw back from the brink and to design, build and allow to happen something that can actually go on – and go on in the direction of increasingly shared prosperity and increasingly contributed collaboration? The recalling of our institutions to, or their redesigning for, their essential purposes of promoting human survival and flourishing are no longer a matter of 'fine tuning' or the inevitable ups and downs of history or a set of different and discrete struggles in differing parts of the world. There is now one world, one 'we' and one future. Is there any chance of organizing and responding accordingly? And are there any resources beyond our own resources to assist us in this and to offer us this exciting prospect and possibility?

For the issue is not simply survival. The strands of argument and experience which compel us to face the issue of God and which bind this issue to the discoveries and demands of being one human and global 'we' include much more than the distressing negativities in which religious people in practice contradict the godliness of their claimed God and the threatening negativities in both institutions and uses of the resources of the world which question our survival. Just as behind, beyond and within the confusions of religion there are the positive and compelling glimpses of the enthralling and the enticing glory of God, so behind, beyond and within the struggles, confusions and threats of human society and human institutions there are positive and compelling glimpses of the demands and offers and achievements of human persons, human potentialities, human loving and human sharing. Our struggles and searches, our anxieties and hopes, our fears and our longings are not just about survival. They are much more positive than that, for somewhere in the midst of it all and pointing beyond it all there is an offer which goes deeper and is more compelling than all the threats, and a provoking promise which challenges all pessimism, despair and apathy.

This is the issue of God (or the issue of God is one form of this central human issue) which is compounded of glimpses of the glory of God; the pressures of the betrayal of God by religion, paralleled by the betrayal of humanity by our institutions; the negative pressures of the threats of our destroying our environment and ourselves; and the deep positive pressures of the possibilities of love, community, collaboration and celebration. These pressures, both of problems and threats recognized, and of glories and promises glimpsed, compel and invite us into the middle of what is going on in human and social living at all levels, from the intimately personal, through the shaping effects of structures and institutions, to the ultimately global – and to the visions and promises beyond, which must nevertheless be seen in the midst. So the transcendent visions and promises must be sought and responded to in the particularities. That, I believe, is where God sends us and that is where God is to be found. That, I further believe, is the functional meaning of the Christian faith and claim that Jesus is 'God with us'. Moreover, since Jesus is, for us Christians, the focussing and functional declaration of God's identity and intention, it follows that the God who sends does not send us as if he were a universal commander-in-chief who equips his subordinates with a master battle-plan for a guaranteed victory. He ('she', 'it') is rather more like a creative artist and a suffering servant who offers the opportunity to collaborate with his passion for the possibilities and mystery of holiness, righteousness and love. Likewise the God we find is not a possession to be made use of for our own ends, our own comfort as we at present perceive it and the glory of our own church, but a support in the struggles, a promise in the searching and a presence to be celebrated while we are on the way. (This implies a much wider interpretation of 'ecumenicity' than we have yet faced up to but that is not discussed anywhere in this particular book.)

So, as a believer in God, or as a very indifferent 'believer' who cannot shake off an inescapable conviction that God has got hold of me – and have no real wish to escape from God – I plunge in to reflect, explore and offer. It is such interim, occasional and insufficiently finished offerings that these pieces are. I have decided to have them published and therefore seek a wider audience for them than those present on the occasions when they were originally delivered because I believe that there are some questions and hints in them which urgently need to be taken into our public and common debates about our future, both as a society and in the whole world. Also I find (or, rather, am found by) an excitement, a hope and a promise which I am bound to attempt to share. God (or more realistically, my glimpses of and belief in God – although there may be some godly gift in them) compels me to be a missionary. God is so glorious and the possibilities of being human, however tantalizing, threatening and threatened they are, yet remain so wonderful and reflective of that glory that the glimpses and the possibilities must be shared.

This means particularities and it means politics. It means also that particular particularities and the way I presented them or referred to them at the time may now seem, in the light of hindsight, to be ill-chosen or ill-presented. But selective re-writing or editorial touching-up would conceal part of the point. This is that in obedience to God glimpsed, and in pursuit of God hoped for, one must get into the midst of what is going on, and this means being at the risk of one's own limited and imperfect perceptions and choices in relation to the limited and imperfect perceptions and choices of others. Sometimes this leads to getting working examples wrong. This does not invalidate the necessity and urgency of the questions being worked at or of the insights being tried out and shaped up. Indeed, the discussions provoked by a perhaps unnecessarily controversially phrased working example may well promote a wider discussion of a necessary and urgent issue than would come about from a rather more judicious formulation. And, in any case, glimpses of a transcendent and gracious God should surely help to maintain a sense of humour which should assist in preventing one taking oneself – or one's mistakes – too seriously. Finally, some of the working examples touched on in these pieces do seem to be realistic and accurate – such as the suggestion in the Hibbert Lecture that the majority of people in this country do not find current political diagnoses and programmes of either the Left or the Right convincing, realistic and hopeful (supported by the General Election voting), or the point in the City of London 1987 Sermon about the instability of the computerized systems programmed to respond to their own responses (compare 'Black Monday' and continuing tremors).

Thus the pieces here, published as they were originally presented, all have political aspects. When and where they were reported in the media it was the obviously political bits which were selected and headlined. A principal reason for publishing them so that they can be read as a whole is to establish the point that they are all primarily *theological* pieces. They are addressed to the issue of God and they are based on material drawn from the biblical and Christian traditions about God. The publication of them as a book would be quite sufficiently worthwhile if it finally put paid to the simplistic (and often self-interested) nonsense that politics and religion should be kept apart. This is quite impossible, because of the nature of human life in society and because of the nature of the God who is portrayed in the Bible and worshipped in the Christian traditions. Of course, how the practices of politics and the pursuit of response to God should interweave and interact is a constant matter for the most careful and sensitive exploration, discussion and experimentation. The pieces in this book are offered as a contribution to that exploration, discussion and practice.

In so far as they do pursue one particular political theme in the narrower sense of 'political' (i.e. in specific relation to party politics and to the formation of governments and government policies and programmes) they are very preliminary explorations into the territory on which a restoration or reinvention of a pragmatic politics is to be found. This would be a pragmatic politics which will be commensurate with the actual demands of survival, flourishing and living together in the twenty-first century and also appropriate for a further advance in democracy. Current party politics offer either a euphoric short-term and short-sighted clarity about global market enterprise which cannot be sustainable very far into the future and might collapse very abruptly, or a confusion of confusions about anything else. This is probably typical of, and symptomatic of, the end of an era – perhaps capitalism and industrialism as ways of life to do with growth and consumption and production have had their two hundred years.

The question is whether we can sufficiently quickly invent, discover and allow to emerge a democratic politics which will both match the demands of the future and actually help to sustain the possibility of there being any future. This could not be an ideological politics because you cannot plot the unknown, or take into account the effects of the as yet unimagined or uninvented. And in any case, we have learnt, and are living with, the harm which ideologies – whether of 'the people' or of 'the Market' do. There may be God and it may be possible to respond to the mystery in the midst of things which can sustain us and move us forward. Or there may be no God and we are on our own in the midst of an indifferent dynamism of process and change. But in either case we require a variety of pragmatic politics which neither expects nor promises too much and which encourages and enables increasing democratic collaboration and participation so that we can together struggle our way forward into a newness which will enable us to survive while becoming better at being the neighbour, better at sustaining community, better at exercising a responsible stewardship of the earth and better at cherishing, developing and sharing sustainable and enjoyable worth.

From my perspective this is an attempt to w.
times and for our society and for our one earth
should, in practice, love God, love our neighbour and
the earth which he has given us for the flourishing of all.

For the record it should perhaps be set down that the pieces
which follow were first delivered as follows:

1. The Cost of Hope – a sermon preached at my enthronement as Bishop of Durham in Durham Cathedral, 21
   September 1984
2. The Necessities and Limits of the Market – address to
   the Annual Meeting of the Bristol Industrial Mission held
   in Bristol Cathedral, 4 March 1986
3. Why an Industry Year? – Sermon preached at St Martins-
   in-the-Fields, London, for the annual service of the London
   Industrial Chaplaincy, 28 May 1986
4. The City of London – New Year Sermon for the City
   preached at St Michael's, Cornhill, 13 January 1987
5. Christian Doctrine: The Challenge to and from Poverty –
   Address to the First National Conference of Church
   Action on Poverty, November 1982
6. The Church, the Inner City and the Wilderness – Sacred
   Trinity Lecture delivered in Trinity Church, Salford, 15
   November 1986
7. Faith in the City – Presidential Address to the Synod of
   the Diocese of Durham, 2 May 1987
8. The God of Freedom and the Freedom of God – 1985
   Hibbert Lecture broadcast by BBC Radio 4, 14 April
   1985
9. Prospects for Peace – City of Durham Annual Lecture
   given in Durham City Town Hall, 11 April 1985
10. How Green is our Future? – Lunchtime address at St
    James's Piccadilly, 2 November 1987

PART ONE

Politics, Economics and Industry

1

The Cost of Hope

May the God of hope fill you with all joy and peace by your faith in him until, by the power of the Holy Spirit, you overflow with hope.
(Romans 15. 13)

We could do with some help from this 'God of hope' here in the North East. Unemployment is at thirty-five to fifty per cent. They propose to dump radioactive waste on us as if we were the scrap-yard of Britain. The miners' strike highlights how divided and distressed society is, to the point of violence. Christians seem absorbed in bad-tempered arguments about belief, or marriage, or politics. The organized churches find financial problems looming larger and larger. We all wonder if the old men in the Kremlin or in the White House will over reach themselves and actually use the nuclear weapons which are unthinkable but real. If you stop and think, hope does not come easily.

But we are stopped here in this great and moving building to enthrone a Bishop of Durham. This is a questionable business too. Of the person involved, it can evidently be said that he is not everyone's cup of tea and that he has even been accused of being some people's cup of poison. Of the procedures, we are told that 'enthronement' is an ancient symbol of the bishop's task and privilege to care for and 'chair' the diocese. A 'throne' is just a chair. Nonetheless, being installed in what is repeatedly claimed to be 'the highest throne in Christendom' leaves the representative relationship between a Lord Bishop of Durham and the Lord Jesus Christ inevitably ambiguous.

Further, the very title 'Bishop of Durham' has its problems. My welcome at Darlington yesterday and the representative nature of the gathering here tonight make it clear that the Bishop of Durham is still regarded as just that, i.e. the Bishop who will stand for and serve the whole of the County of Durham, indeed, the whole of the North East. Here I see no ambiguity. If such opportunities for service and representation are open to me, then I am wholly committed to them. The God and Father of the Lord Jesus Christ is the God who is concerned for all and at one with all. It is the hope and task of his church to long for, and to work for, his acknowledgment as God by all. But we do not wait for that acknowledgment before we seek to serve all, any more than God waited to send his Son to die for all. The ambiguity is elsewhere. What part does the Church of England diocese of Durham now actually play in the ordinary life of the area? Further, the Church of England by no means contains all of the Christians there are in the area. So, being called 'Bishop of Durham' and acquiring a territorial signature verges on the pretentious and the anachronistic. Is this great building itself a magnificent symbol of past history or a sign of power for the future?

I face you, therefore, as an ambiguous, compromised and questioning person entering upon an ambiguous office in an uncertain church in the midst of a threatened and threatening world. I dare to do this and I even, with fear and trembling, rejoice to do this because this is where God is to be found. In the midst, that is, of the ambiguities, the compromises, the uncertainties, the questions and the threats of our daily and ordinary worlds. For the church exists, despite all its failings

4

and all its historically acquired clutter, because the disturbing, provocative, impracticable, loving and utterly God-centred Jesus got himself crucified. Then God vindicated this God-centred way of life, love and being by raising Jesus up. So the disillusioned disciples were turned into spirit-filled apostles and the church has ever since been learning and re-learning that in the flesh and blood of this man is God's way of being with us, and of giving us a share in the bringing in of his kingdom. If we long for hope, then we must not fall back on hoping against hope and refusing to face ordinary realities, within us and around us, both in society and in the church. Nor must we indulge in cheap hope, expecting miracle solutions either from God or from politicians. For we know that keeping hope alive in this sort of a world cost God the cross.

The cost of hope for us, therefore, is to get rid of all triumphalism and false expectations and to stay with our problems in the power of God and in search of God who is waiting for us and looking for us. If we who are Christians can work this out in the church and in our religious practices, then we shall also be ready to help to work this out also in society at large and in our community practices. Let me try and explain.

Because the God who gives himself for us in Jesus Christ and also gives himself to us in the Spirit is so glorious, so gracious and so promising, we Christians are always liable to expect things of him which are contrary to his revealed character and ways of working. God has committed himself to the risk of creation, the identification of incarnation and the perseverance of indwelling. His principal and unique declaration of himself to us is in Jesus, whom we Christians recognize as Christ. There was a glimpse of glory in the transfiguration, but the fulfilling of the transfiguring glory was the disfiguring of the cross. The resurrection did not avoid rejection, desolation and death. It was brought about through them and out of them. If God goes that way, we can expect no short cuts. We have no right to expect a church which will guarantee us infallible comfort, a Bible which will assure us of certain truth, charismatic experiences which settle our knowledge of God for good and all, miracles which prove God's presence beyond a doubt, questions which we are quite sure must always be put, or insights into the kingdom of God which assuredly promise social utopias. We forget again and again that in discovering the resurrection some doubted (Matt. 28.17); at the first Pentecost some asked 'What can this mean?' but others said contemptuously, 'They have been drinking!' (Acts 2. 13); while at the transfiguration Peter was both frightened and confused. God does not impose himself, he gives himself, and our faith, interpretation and obedience are always required to discern him and respond to him.

Of course we do have the church to support us, the Bible to judge and renew us, experiences of the Spirit which kindle in us transformation, assurance and joy, miracles which encourage and direct people of faith, questions which we must ask as long as we acknowledge the limitations of the intellect, and a call to relate the kingdom of God to what is going on in our society. But God must never be identified with his gifts or the occasions of his giving. Above all he does not give us these gifts, of catholicity, of Bible, of charismata, of miracle, of intellect and of social concern for us variously and differently to make party labels of them and to set Catholic against Protestant, against Evangelical, against charismatic, against liberal, against activist. We must be making a mistake about God if we insist that the chief ways in which we personally experience God's gifts and his giving are his only ways or *the* definitive ways. The greatness, the glory and the freedom of God relativizes all our disputes.

Christian conflicts, therefore, are not about the who, but about the how. *Whom* we serve is the one and only God known to us through Jesus Christ in the Spirit. *How* we serve is a necessary but secondary matter, and whatever the answers in practice and in theory, they are always subordinate to him, and inadequate for him. So none of our ways of understanding God and serving God are strictly speaking, *God's* ways. All are *our* ways which he allows us responsibly and humbly to develop and then submit to his blessing, his judgment, his renewal and, sometimes, his reversal. The cost of hope in renewing the church, spreading Christian discipleship and growing in Christian unity is the relativizing of us all by the greatness of his glory and by the greatness of the risks which he takes in his love, so that we are set free for new forms of obedience, fresh discoveries of his grace and new ways of working together despite our differences.

This offer of freedom for newness and hope under the almightiness of God and through the down-to-earth presence of God is not however, by any means confined to Christian churches and religious affairs. There is a power and a possibility here about hope in our present social discontents. Here again, triumphalism, absolutism and illusions have to be got rid of if we are to find hopeful and human ways forward. The cost of hope in our society and our politics is a responsible readiness for compromise. Once we are clear that nobody has God's view of things or does God's will in God's way, then it also becomes clear that to insist on one's own view and nothing but one's own view and the whole of one's own view is outrageously self–righteous, deeply inhuman and damnably dangerous. It is to set our inevitable conflicts on course for destructive fights which no one can win, through which all will lose and which could end by destroying us all. Until we reach the kingdom of God, responsible mutually worked-out compromise will again and again be of the essence both of true godliness and true humanity. Anyone who rejects compromise as a matter of policy, programme or conviction is putting himself or herself in the place of God, and Christians and atheists can surely be agreed that, whether there is a God or not, no person or set of persons from our human race is suitable for divine appointment. Consider the bearing of this on our most pressing current social tragedy, the miners' strike.

It suggests that there must be no *victory* in the miners' strike. There must be no victory, but a speedy settlement which is a compromise pointing to community and the future.

There must be no victory, because the miners must not be defeated. They are desperate for their communities and this desperation forces them to action. No one concerned in this strike, and we are *all* concerned, must forget for one moment what it is like to be part of a community centred on a mine or a works when that mine or works closes. It is death, depression and desolation. A society which seeks economic progress for material ends must not indifferently exact such human suffering from some for the affluence of others. The miners, then, must not be defeated, and this must be the first priority.

But there must be no victory for them on present terms because these include negotiation on their terms alone, pits left open at all costs and the endorsement of civil violence for group ends. Yet, equally, there must be no victory for the government. This government, whatever it says, seems in action to be determined to defeat the miners and thus treat workers as not part of 'us'. They also seem to be indifferent to poverty and powerlessness. Their financial measures consistently improve the lot of the already better off while worsening that of the badly off. Their answer to civil unrest seems to be to make the means of suppression more efficient while ignoring or playing down the causes. Such a government cannot promote community or give hope in the very difficult days we are faced with. It cannot even effectively promote the genuine insights it has about the need for realism in what is economically possible. To wish a victory over the miners is simply to store up trouble not to reduce it.

8

And there must be no victory for 'us', that is to say, society at large in our various groupings, who by our trends, tendencies and voting set up the sort of materialistic and consumer society we have. There will be no new hope for the future if all we get is the end of the strike and therefore, apparently, a quiet life again and the assurances that 'they' are dealing with things. Our problems will not go away. We shall find hope only if more and more of us are prepared to face up to what is going on, what is wrong in it, and what might be brought out of it.

Therefore, a negotiated settlement which is compromise and demands of us *all* further work on the problems both of the miners and of society at large is the only hopeful thing. But how might this come about? Might it be by Mr Macgregor withdrawing from his chairmanship and Mr Scargill climbing down from his absolute demands? The withdrawal of an imported elderly American to leave a reconciling opportunity for some local product is surely neither dishonourable nor improper. It would show that the interpretation of his appointment as the provocation of the miners to fight in order that they might be defeated was false, and it would indicate that the government values the cost of hope as much as or more than the fruit of victory. After all, victory leaves hurt and more trouble. Hope has a future. But this would have to be matched by evidence that Mr Scargill, too, was not an absolutist but a compassionate and realistic negotiator who cares more for people and for the future than for an ideology. Without withdrawal and without climbing down it looks as if we are faced with several people determined to play God. And this gives us all hell

However this may be, and whatever may happen in the immediate future, the direction of the life of any branch or section of the Christian church is clear. The direction is God. This is the God who has already paid the cost of hope in this

9

confusing, risky but potentially glorious and often enjoyable world. He it is who is as he is in Jesus, identified with our flesh and blood, ready to meet us through his Spirit wherever there is human need or despair, human creativity or joy. What we have to do is to face up to what is going on, get involved in what is going on and discern him in what is going on. His gift will be himself, his promise will be the growth of all that is human and his power will be hope. And in the midst of it all our anchor and assurance will be to worship him, to wait for him and to rest in him. So 'may the God of hope fill you with all joy and peace by your faith in him until, by the power of the Holy Spirit, you overflow with hope'.

2

The Necessities and the Limits of the Market

Some people may think that I am being unnecessarily provocative and political in taking as my subject a discussion of the Market. What has this to do with God? Further, what special insights or, indeed, ordinary competence allows or encourages a bishop publicly to tackle this subject? A major purpose of mine here is to show why arguments about economic policy and the Market are, in practice and at the present time, inevitably arguments which raise issues of faith and which require and demand theological reflections. I also hope to show that this means that Christians as such need to be ready to face up to and enter into these arguments. I start from the role that is given to something called 'the Market' by those who are arguing for both the necessity and the morality of the economic policies of the present government. A good and, I believe, typical example of this type of argument is contained in the first leader of *The Times* 13 February 1986 entitled 'Over the Horizon', which sets out to discuss the aftermath of the Westland affair.

But while the dust and the noise suggest a diversity of future options for Britain, the reality that there are only two fundamental choices remains hidden. . . There can either be a strengthening of the opportunities of the individual that

Mrs Thatcher has pioneered, the further rolling back of the State, the increasing demands on personal responsibilities; or there can be the opposite – more State intervention, the sapping of individual will, the easy conditions of corrosive national decline.

What has been learnt under Mrs Thatcher, the leader goes on, is 'that the creation of wealth is not an automatic process'. There is now a tendency to argue that we should start going slow and mixing state power back into our ways of going on.

Mrs Thatcher's model of society, on the other hand, is quite different. It is one in which a large number of individual decisions are governed by the forces of the market place and set in motion by the free choices of people who have a stake in the wealth of the nation.

Here we have a clear statement of what might be called 'the current Conservative Quadrilateral'. This consists of the individual – free choices – in and under the market – which produces wealth. I shall come back to this.

Finally, there is a series of references to the benefits and the benefitted people arising from this approach.

While worker's living standards have been rising, inflation is now understood for the cruel and unfair tax on ordinary people's savings that is... a massive extension of home ownership and share ownership have been achieved... Every new shareholder has a chance to join the ranks of those in society who earn their living from their capital as well as from their labour... Every new householder gains an asset which could be used to produce wealth as well as shelter... The prize is an increase in the number of people who are liberated from psychological dependence on the State, who are prepared to consider private provision for education and health care, whose new freedoms help the process of

12

defining where the State's responsibilities should end and how they should be paid for. Wealth does not need to be more widely spread, it needs to be seen and felt to be more widely spread. Individuals need to be encouraged to keep the wealth to themselves.

We note in this last sentiment the echo of Mr Gladstone, who said that wealth should fructify in the pockets of the people.

The picture here is clearly articulated and consistent. I hope you can already see why we are embarked upon an exploration of faith and theology and not just engaged in a political, still less a party-political, discussion. For what is being set out is a statement about the way things are, about what is best for human beings and about overall aims of society. We are clearly in the business of a way of looking at the world as a whole, of an evaluation of human beings and of morality. This becomes even clearer if we look quickly to other pieces from *The Times*. First, an article of 11 February 1986 by Roger Scruton entitled 'Science with No Time for Facts'. This is an attack on economists, during which the author writes;

> And if 'monetarism' is appealing it is not, I believe, because of its scientific credentials but because of its moral truth. . . Common morality tells us that prudence is a virtue, and that trust should neither be exploited nor betrayed. It would have reminded the banker that the dollars which he loaned the governments that have not given the slightest evidence of their probity were not his to lend, that he held them in trust.

He concludes:

> We may not be able to solve the problem of unemployment, but perhaps we could at least understand it were we to refuse the terms which economists recommend to us and to trust instead the language of morality.

13

The plea for morality is echoed in an article of 15 February 1986 discussing the problems of blacks in the inner cities of the United States by John O'Sullivan entitled 'Victims in Need of Virtue'. Among other things, he writes:

> The British sociologist Christie Davies points out that there was a similar increase in crime, illegitimacy and social disorder in early nineteenth-century Britain. But it was solved very differently. The Victorian élite tackled these problems successfully by gradually imbuing all classes with a morality. . . which had as its central tenet the idea that each individual was morally responsible for his own behaviour. This morality helped to create the British working-class with its ethic of respectability.

He finishes by writing:

> There is no effective substitute for Victorian values – namely holding young blacks accountable for their actions. But how many people in the American élite have that kind of courage?

You will note the now explicit reference to 'Victorian values' and remember the echo of Mr Gladstone in the leader I started from. We are clearly and explicitly being presented with a call to return to the values of late nineteenth-century liberal *laissez-faire*. It is surely legitimate to wonder whether this is really a good and realistic way of looking forward or whether we are still under the spell of a form of backward-looking nostalgia.

However that may be, we are given a clearly argued exposition of the line of argument we are considering in a lecture entitled 'Monetarism and Morality' (published 1985 by the Centre for Policy Studies) by Professor Brian Griffiths, who it will be remembered is Mrs Thatcher's economic adviser. He is also a concerned and committed Christian. The second section of Professor Griffith's lecture provides an invaluable clarification for various uses of the term 'monetarism' which ought to be compulsory reading for anyone who is concerned with what we are now discussing. His whole argument needs to be taken very seriously, but I am just going to take two or three quotations from his third section (entitled 'Morality'). First,

> What is not commonly recognized is that inflation is at heart a moral problem, because inflation is theft. As Keynes forcefully argues in his *Tract on Monetary Reform*, inflation is a form of concealed taxation. It is a tax levied on the holders of money balances...
>
> Control of inflation is... therefore, based on the moral principle that such capriciousness at the heart of the economy is incompatible with justice; not only that, it is difficult to see on moral grounds how any government can be content to consent to a permanent positive rate of inflation, in the knowledge that in issuing currency it is misleading its citizens as to what its 'promise to pay' really amounts to. There is a second and equally important moral strand in the Government's medium term financial strategy; it is the attempt to move away from the corporate state and to enhance the economic position of the individual in the context of the family.
>
> Underlying these policies is a moral concern: to encourage and develop private ownership by families, whether of their own homes or of the firms in which they work, and to enable people to pursue their jobs free of the restriction of monopolistic trade unions. As such they constitute a fundamental step forward in the creation of a more responsible and healthy society.

Professor Griffiths is clear that the present level of unemployment is totally unsatisfactory and discusses this separately. I shall also return to this. He concludes the present part of his argument:

15

However, not only is the policy just and sustainable, it is also participatory. It is not participatory in the sense of accepting the politicization of economic life, of supporting the development of the corporate state – but rather it is an attempt to encourage direct participation of individuals and families in the economy through ownership.

We note again the powerful connection between individuals, freedom of choice and both morality and market efficiency.

I hope therefore that I have sufficiently shown the wide-ranging implications of what I have called the Conservative Quadrilateral of 1. the individual; 2. choice; 3. the market; 4. wealth; and why it is necessary as a general matter of humanity and faith to consider 'the necessities and the limits of the Market'. I want to continue the investigation by considering the people who are referred to as developing and flourishing under the supposed social and economic reality. They may be listed from the material I have already used as follows: ordinary people with savings or the holders of money balances; home owners; shareholders; people who are prepared to consider private provision of education and health care; establishers of small businesses; and, more generally, those who participate in the economy and in society through ownership. Freedom for these people means having enough resources and stability through ownership to be able, to a very considerable extent, to choose what they want for themselves and for their families across the widest possible range of choices. These choices, from shopping on Sunday to obtaining education and health care, should, to the greatest extent possible, be exercised in and controlled in their effects by the Market.

I do not think that it is an obviously and purely party-political move to raise a question at this point: 'But what about the several millions of our fellow citizens who have no prospects whatever, either immediately, or in a medium-term

16

foreseeable future, of taking part in this type of sufficiently-resourced participation in an ownership democracy?' It *may* be that 'there is no alternative', owing to something like 'the nature of things', 'economic realities' and so on. But one has to be pretty careful before coming finally, positively and practically to that conclusion. Christian faith might have squarely to face the question 'Is the world really like this in its entirety?', 'Do we have to accept this diagnosis of reality?' Of course, in facing such questions all concerned Christians would also have to face the hard questions about hard facts to do with technical monetarism, market operations and wealth production as well as wealth distribution.

There is an additional reason for equipping ourselves to wrestle with questions like these. It is that many of the people who put forward the arguments and policies built up around what I am nicknaming 'the current Conservative Quadrilateral', – the individual, free choice; market; wealth – do very well out of these policies. Of course, enough people must do well enough out of some policies or another for a society to be viable, but we surely need to exercise caution and self-examination, especially when it still seems to be the case that even when the economy is said to be going reasonably well, a very considerable number of people are doing badly or even doing worse than they were doing. I cannot help feeling that the very serious moral dilemma, which is not faced up to adequately by the morality we have so far been discussing, is focussed in the increasing flourishing of the 'haves' and the increasing deprivation of the 'have nots'. This is illustrated for me by the contrast between the following.

In the debate in General Synod on the report *Faith in the City*, the then Dean of St Paul's, Alan Webster, referred to a newsletter from a big firm of City stockbrokers which reported that the average income of their executives was £47,000 per annum (leaving aside stock options and the like). How does this fit in with all the people in my diocese and in the North East generally (as well as elsewhere) who, already dependent on Social Security and with no chance of employment, seem bound to find themselves even worse off after Mr Fowlers Review? I do not think that this is just an emotive and a 'wet' question. It shows up a structural deficiency or inefficiency which requires very tough and very persistent thinking and a good deal of courage and vision in following through the consequences of such thinking. It is indeed a challenge to faith.

It is questions like these which force us to pursue the issue of the limits of the Market. Another one, of course connected with what I have already talked about, is the question of structural unemployment. This a vast subject in itself, but I would like just to refer to Professor Griffiths' references to this in the penultimate part of his lecture. He refers to structural unemployment of three million or so and then says:

> This level of unemployment is not the result of any law of economics but simply of institutional practices in the labour market. Unemployment at this level, however, is intolerable in human terms and clearly must be addressed by policy makers. It cannot be changed by reflationary policies or even by achieving a policy of price stability. It can only be reduced by reforming the institutional practices of the labour market.

I assume that this means that if people out of work are flexible enough about the wages they would take and the jobs they would do then 'the labour market' would clear and we should get rid of structural unemployment (although by no means all unemployment). The problem here seems to be that there is no reason why 'the Market', that is, the set of places where supply meets demand, with prices and costs which balance out and enable profits, should actually suffice 'the labour market'. Surely one at any rate of our problems is that with foreseeable, sustainable and resourced demand, we do not need to employ many of the people who are, or are coming on to, the labour market? One of the clearest evidences of the limits of the Market may be that it cannot guarantee, in present circumstances, sufficient demand for labour to clear 'the labour market' We may have no obvious ways, as yet, of tackling this problem, but we may well make it worse if, for the sort of reasons (including moral reasons) which I have been looking at earlier, we 'put our faith in the Market'. It seems reasonable and prudent, therefore, to ask ourselves: 'How much faith should we have in the Market?' It seems also that Christians should be particularly ready to risk asking a question like this, even if it does not straight away lead us to practical answers, because Christians are sure that real human hope and possibility lies in God and not in any particular set of circumstances or theories. So we can risk facing real questions which do not yet have applicable answers.

The first to 'How much faith should we have in the Market?' would seem to be 'None whatever'. For on consideration there is no such thing. It is a theoretical abstraction to do with an interacting set of market and other circumstances. Further, even if it existed, it would not be a proper object of faith but simply some set of facts and parameters. It is surely important that 'the Market' should be something which we can handle, not something which controls us. Secondly, even if 'the Market' is a very serious theoretical concept, there is surely the problem that 'for the economist the real world is always a special case'. Talk about the Market, however highly analytical and carefully constructed, is a way of getting to grips with the real world and how it affects us and seeking to alter this, but not something which wholly defines the situation. This is where we may return to our suspicion about people who promote talk about the Market. Are they arguing about undoubted realities or are they to some extent arguing about their

19

own interests? Thirdly, is it prudent and sustainable to have 'the Market' as our main model about our world for the future? What of competition as the main force in a world which we increasingly find to be closed? It looks economically as if the Market and competition are largely kept going by a process of leap-frogging and skimming-off. Those who can get the cheapest labour and the brightest ideas exploit for a bit until they themselves are driven out by others. This does have certain motivating and innovatory effects. But it also has many other bad side-effects, and one begins to wonder how long it is sustainable, especially if we join it up to the whole notion of the world as an ecologically closed system with resources which have to be used at a controlled rate. Might we not have to repent of too much marketing?

Then there are other questions which take us back into the previous discussion, such as the inadequacies of what is usually called 'the trickle-down theory'. That is to say, the production of wealth 'at the top' does not trickle down all that efficiently and sometimes does not trickle down at all. We have the problems of the divisions within the Third World and between the Third World and others. We have a problem, increasingly recognized in our country, of 'two nations': this tendency to increase a separation between the successful with chances and the unsuccessful with no chances. This sort of thing calls in question too narrow a definition of the individual and of freedom of choice. There are also the well–known questions which Keynes tackled, maybe over-optimistically, about how you get on if you concentrate only on the supply side. Where does the necessary demand side come from? And why should it be supposed that the Market will clear itself at a level which is at all appropriate for human and social issues, or indeed for human and social survival? It looks, therefore, as if there are considerable arguments for attempting to subordinate 'the Market' to a broader and, in the long run, more practical view of the way in which we should hope both to let our society run and enable it to run.

But, finally, we may well be inclined to say 'this is all too difficult and uncertain. Let us get back to some simple faith which will enable each one of us as Christians to live with integrity and hope within all these difficult and confusing things which we cannot possibly hope either to handle or influence.' I would like to close, therefore, by giving a very brief outline of what I see as involved in being a Christian. As a Christian I believe that *Jesus is Lord*. This means that this historical person Jesus of Nazareth embodies that ultimate mystery which has the last word about everything. To use one of the strands of biblical language, what is seen and done and achieved in him is what 'lords it' over the universe, that is, keeps it as a universe (or universe of universes) and ensures that it has a pattern and will fulfil a purpose. Jesus is and points to the ultimately dominating feature of all things. That is to say, Jesus is, in history, the decisive clue to and the expression of God. Indeed, Jesus is not about Christianity, he is about God.

This is quite clear from the New Testament, including the Synoptic Gospels with all their talk of the kingdom of God and the Gospel of John with its talk by Jesus of 'I and my Father'. If one believes 'Jesus is Lord', then one is irrevocably committed to the business of God.

Now what is this business of God? It is his whole work of creation, redemption and fulfilment. One way of putting it in New Testament terms is to say that the business of God is the manifestation, the building up and the completing of his kingdom. This is the 'Our Father' prayer which Jesus taught us.

Can we strip this language and imagery down to some simple formula to enable us to relate this faith in God to the economic and other goings-on of which we are a part? I would suggest as one way: what Jesus Christ shows us Christians is that *God is* and he is for us. We are part of a divine and cosmic project wherein and whereby God will bring it about that everything and everyone that is willing shares in him without interruption, distortion or diminution. This is the kingdom of heaven – where God is God and God is shared without interruption, distortion or diminution. That is why the kingdom of heaven came in Jesus who was wholly one with God in the circumstances of his time and our world. We need to remember that this turned out to be crucifying, so we cannot have any easily utopian or smooth comfortable hopes about either the practice or the results of following Jesus in this world.

Nevertheless, as Jesus is our definite clue to God, we know that God is and that he is for us both cosmically and particularly. The mystery which underlies, overarches, interpenetrates and lies ahead of everything is all-embracing, and therefore not to be privatized. And yet at the same time and as such there is the assertion and offer and development of all individuals who are persons, privately, personally and relationally and socially. Therefore all women and men are potentially able to share, and meant to share, in that cosmic worth which is Love. We are called to be sons and daughters of the kingdom, children of the kingdom, co-heirs of the kingdom, fellow-workers in the kingdom. So when we are faced with, or involved in, goings-on which affect men and women we are concerned with the business of God which is to do with establishing the worth of women and men in, and in relation to, the kingdom of God. This being so, how can we avoid wrestling with those economic realities and those claims, necessities, and limits about the Market which so much affect all of us both immediately as well as corporately?

3

Why an Industry Year?

A society which needs to promote an *Industry Year* is clearly either in a muddle or in a mess or both. Is it not obvious that without a sufficient, efficient and profitable range of industrial activities a society cannot be sustained, let alone maintained, as civilized and caring? Surely, therefore, it is obvious that there is a necessity and a calling to be *industrious* – to work at providing the means for maintaining life and for living it at the best standards we can achieve. So why do we have to organize to combat an 'anti-industrial culture' (as so much of the Industry Year literature points out we have to). We must indeed be confused, uncertain and incoherent! Fancy having to campaign to convince people that it is a good thing to earn our living – and a better thing to earn a good living. *Of course*, wealth must be produced before it can be enjoyed and this is what industry is for. So why Industry Year?

Clearly there is more to this than meets the eye, and we must look for some possible sources of this confusion and uncertainty. I would like to start from something I have noticed in reading what I have seen of Industry Year literature and propaganda. One notices that this propaganda is directed to getting people interested in being managers or skilled technicians and so on and does not really address itself to what, in the old days at any rate, one would have called the 'industrial hands'. When we were having a discussion in diocesan synod about Industry Year and people were asked to write down their quick and spontaneous reactions to the notion of 'industry', what one small group produced was 'boredom and noise'. There is not much reference to this in Industry Year propaganda. And if it is pointed out that we are well on the way to doing away with all this because of things like robots, then we have to bear in mind that of course the robots are doing away with the employment. So we begin to see that there are plenty of problems in the productive processes and in the relationship of industry to and in society.

These problems range fairly widely. For example, industry with us is now very closely, if not entirely, related to talk and concern about markets and competition. Yet there is a real question here. Competitive complexes are inherently unstable, both structurally and systematically. The whole point about competition is that it should necessarily succeed by defeating other less competitive complexes. It is therefore bound to be a series of leap-frogs and dog-eats-dog, and the whole thing cannot but be unstable. It may be that this is to be held in stability by the attempt to build up multi-nationals. But then we have some other very grave problems, both about whether size beyond a certain point is efficient in relation to most wealth-producing and humanly worth-while activities, and about how we are to deal with great complexes that are more powerful than many national states. In any case, it is clear that competitive industry is bound regularly to produce obsolescence. This obsolescence will be concentrated in particular areas which will then become unrenewable under the current terms by which the system is operating. This sort of thing is very much before my eyes in the North East. It is further declared that the system cannot afford to provide for the care and renewal of such areas in any adequate way, at any rate at the moment.

Then we have to consider that whatever anyone may say, there are very strict limits to growth. These limits exist not only through the possibilities of consumption of non-renewable resources or the consumption of resources at a faster rate than they can be renewed but also in the area that has been drawn attention to by that very important book by Fred Hirsch entitled *Social Limits to Growth* which points out that there are a whole lot of things that people enjoy which, if they are enjoyed by more than so many people, cease to be enjoyable or even to exist. Consumption in a worthwhile way is simply not indefinitely extensible. Which leads on to the broader questions of ecology, including problems of pollution as well as exhaustion of resources, and problems that are now very sharply highlighted for us by the nuclear dilemma.

Then we have to go on to consider who meets the *social* costs and how they are met. Our economy may be doing well, but literally millions of people are not, and show a good many signs of doing steadily worse. A small example of the problems in this area may be seen in the matter of occupational pensions. If there is pressure to move in the direction of occupational pensions and remove pressure from the State system, how is this related to the very likely fact that a substantial minority of people are not going to be regularly employed or employed at all and so have no paid occupations by which they can earn pensions? One has also, of course, to list the point that for many people 'industry' means a source of jobs, not a source of profits. And industry as a source of jobs is steadily shrinking. It is clear, therefore, that we have to do some very hard rethinking about the relationship between employment and work occupation. It does not look as though a flourishing industri*al* society is necessarily industri*ous*, at least for very many people, so we are then confronted with the question; 'Well, what is *wealth*?'

In this area we have to consider the worries that arise about the distortion of production and profit-making through high-powered marketing methods. Are we really contributing to wealth and welfare by persuading people to buy things which they would never have dreamt they needed if somebody had not conned them into it?

The inter-relation between industry, wealth and society is therefore not all that simple. In particular we may simply have to ask the question: 'What is industry for?'. The current answer seems to be 'to make profits', and then to claim that this is the way and the only way of providing the means for everything else that society requires. But, quite honestly and simply, and apart from any ideology, we are obliged to ask 'Will it work?' The answer would appear to be that it will work for some and for a bit. But it will not work for a significant (and apparently growing) minority. And there are grounds for wondering whether in the long run it will go on working at all. Then the question arises: 'But what *else* is there?' We have heard it on quite good and powerful authority that 'there is no alternative'. But the allegation that there is no alternative does not constitute proof that what we are trying will actually work, and if you cannot answer the question satisfactorily, it may be that you are asking the wrong one or asking it in the wrong form. Now, this is a service of worship for Industry Year and a Christian service at that. So we can ask, and indeed we are required to ask, an overtly theological question. The most obvious one in this context would seem to be 'What are human beings for?' Is the answer that what they are for is to get jobs *in* industry and to obtain consumption *from* industry? So, again, we are confronted with the question whether this will do or whether it will work. That is to ask whether there is any chance of really thus sustaining a viable society which is on its way to increasingly shareable happiness that is of value to more and more people. It is because I believe that we are *in practice* faced with fundamental questions that I have led the argument of the sermon in this direction, and that I also suggested the two lessons which were read for this service (Jeremiah 31.29–34; II Corinthians 5.11–21).

It may be thought that these rather sweepingly theological passages from the Old and New Testaments are remote from Industry Year and its pressing and practical concerns. I think not. It would, however, take more than one sermon to show this, and clearly I have to be careful not to make this sermon too long. However, I would like to consider this argument briefly, and then I will close with suggestions about some indications of lines of activity for Industrial Mission which seem to me to follow from this.

Thus I would suggest that for the practical and political running of our society at present we are sharply confronted with the question 'What are men and women for?' The passages which we have heard read suggest, among other things, that men and women are meant to know God intimately, within themselves and between themselves and for themselves. They also suggest that men and women are for being reconciled to one another. The claim is that all of them are meant to share in this reconciliation in order to be with one another and with God so that through God they may enjoy an infinity of love, worthwhileness, glory and sharing in a worth-while, indeed an eternally worth-while, society. These far-reaching and godly claims clearly make certain suggestions which are relevant to our public, political and industrial dilemmas.

For example, as R.H. Tawney remarks somewhere in developing an argument about industrial relations: 'since even quite common men have souls...'! There is a lot more to human relationships, industrial management, what people really want to consume for and what they want to be in society for and what they can expect to get out of being in society, than straight-forward issues of cost-accounting, profit, consumption and so on. Then the biblical passages I have chosen point to the claim that the only indestructible and infinitely extensible good is enjoyable, supportive and creative relationships. Anything less may tend to lead to zero-sum games, endless fragmentation and conflicts and general deterioration and apathy – if not despair and destruction. The very existence of the sort of claims about the knowledge of God and the reconciling power of God made in the passages from Jeremiah and II Corinthians in fact face us with the question: 'O.K. – when the chips are down, what *is* at work in our world and in our society?' Is there a power at the heart of things who makes for good and who confronts, judges and absorbs what makes for bad, and is available as Spirit, to support struggles for good, confront the work of evil and to renew people in the struggle and innovate hopefully? Or has big industry finally taken over and does unsustainable and basically selfish consumption, much of it frivolous and trivial, as well as often obscenely and inhumanly wasteful, have the last word?

This is a simple and basic issue of faith. It is certainly a simple and basic issue for all who claim to be Christian, for all who believe that the God pointed to in the Bible is really there and really God. Do we believe in this presence at the heart of things who is holiness, righteousness and steadfast love?

Suppose we do believe in and worship such a God. Suppose, above all, we worship him as revealed uniquely in Jesus Christ, the man who is God with us, the man who is God in our flesh and blood, the man who suffers, confronts and overcomes the powers of evil, self-centredness and destruction. Suppose we also believe that this God is known as active and available in the incoming and ongoing Holy Spirit. Then we shall see Industry Year as an opportunity and challenge to work with and within industry to get industry more right in a godly and therefore in a humane direction.

28

This will involve being concerned in constructive criticism and active struggle, of course, to make industry more productive. To waste resources is a bad act of poor stewardship. But it will have to be productive of *real* wealth, that which promotes welfare of people, and the sustainability of the world. It will also have to be concerned with the production of responsible wealth. We simply cannot afford any sort of production if we are to keep a sustainable, viable and hopeful society and world. There have to be various forms of discipline. Moreover all these productive processes will have to be worked out much more sharply in relation to society and in relation to our environment. Far more than lip service will have to be paid to working all this out in relation to the workers in industry. This is clearly a truly formidable challenge. It is made all the more formidable by, for example, the failures of Marxism. Marx and Marxism have produced some very acute and powerful criticisms of the practices of production, but this has not enabled those bringing forth those criticisms and then gaining power to do anything like solving, for example, the problems of production and bureaucracy. Nor have they been any better than anyone else at tackling the problems of production and motivation. Therefore the most powerful critique has not produced an equally powerful solution or way forward. But we are hindered in doing the new thinking that we need to do by the current frightening and unimaginative nostalgia which seems to play such a part in the ideas and the politics of our current society. People seem to wish to turn to nineteenth-century solutions for twenty-first century problems. And yet the nineteenth century solutions did not work all that well even in the nineteenth century and it was necessary to produce counter-criticisms, like those of Marx and countervailing institutions, like trade unions and many other bodies which simply had to come into existence, to protect people who were suffering from the so-called advances and solutions.

Industry Year therefore is a challenge to faith and the church as much as a challenge to industry. We have to ask ourselves whether there is any chance of working out, sweating out, and stumbling on a new symbiosis between industry, society, wealth, and being human in community. Looking at things as they are I certainly cannot be sure that we do have such a chance. But I am bound to make a statement of faith. If God is God and if he is as he is in Jesus Christ and in the Spirit, then there ought to be such a chance. Which is where, I believe, industrial mission, quite possibly in a reconstituted and re-organized form, comes in. Can industrial mission use positions achieved, experiences gained and contacts available for a variety of tasks related to this basic question of whether there is any chance of working out and sweating out a new symbiosis between industry, society, wealth and being human in community?

Tasks, it seems to me, could be found in all, and doubtless more, of the following areas.

First, in bringing together and holding together concerned operatives in industry who are not just concerned, however much they must be, with the particular problems of their particular industry but also have a sense of the wider questions. Such people need to be brought together, held together and sustained in seeking to find the practical importance of the basic and long-term questions to which I have referred. There is something terrifying about the impracticality of the practical man who will not reconsider his practice in the light of changing circumstances and needs. (Of course, the only thing that is equivalent to the terrifying nature of the impracticality of the practical man is the alarming irrelevance of the theoretical man who is not concerned with operation or practice!) We need to be able to show that if we have belief in God then we are ready to face any questions in our concern and care for human beings. There is the further difficulty (as I believe Dorothy

Sayers put it) that, 'most Englishmen would die rather than think and many of them do'. Nonetheless we surely ought to be able to say: 'Put your faith in God and *think*.'

Secondly, ordinary industrialists and ordinary church people (the two classes sometimes overlap!) need to be brought together and sustained in efforts at their own level to look for new ways through developing a new awareness of current realities and using their imagination. We need to develop the notion of small businesses into a much wider range of small-scale efforts at innovation, modification and experiment. We need also to add to the notion of self-help in getting on in a narrowly industrial and profitable way and developing this in the direction of social self-help.

Thirdly, we need to promote and put over pungent and pointed analyses which insist on the necessity of facing these basic questions. For example, people with power, who take or influence decisions, need to be reminded again and again, with as much documentation and evidence as is possible, that whenever you are dealing with a problem there is always more than one set of hard facts. When somebody is attempting to maintain a small business set up on a trading estate and facing the fact that a product can be innovated and established and developed and then itself be overtaken in a period of something like three to five years, of course there is a set of hard facts to deal with the particular marketing and development of that particular product which are the overwhelming hard facts for him. But the hard facts of social deprivation, bad social morale and all the rest of it in the area around the trading estate are just as much hard facts and are as relevant to the development of our society and indeed to what eventually goes on either on the trading estate or in that which replaces it. Those whose ultimate faith is in God and not in any one particular set of human solutions ought to be particularly well qualified to draw attention to those hard facts which hard-pressed persons, whether in industry or government departments, want again and again to ignore. This is part of putting our questions in a wider context from which hopeful and new ways forward might emerge. It is also necessary to press on with these pungent and pointed analyses which go wider than any particular group of interested or expert persons and to do this from a clear basis in faith and theology. This type of criticism must be pursued because it is necessary to show that critics of our current ways of going on are not inevitably Communist or even particularly partisan leftish. We must make a sustained contribution which fights against the uncritical and unthoughtful polarization of discussion into slogans of the right and slogans of the left, most of which are some fifty years or more out of date in any case.

Fourthly, we need to develop sustaining ministries within industry to all who are prepared to suffer and struggle with these wider questions while carrying on their work within industry. It is important to offer such a sustaining ministry because persons who see that the questions which they have to tackle as managers, trainers, trade-union leaders, or trade-union members are nonetheless to be considered in a wider context than that which is defined by their current position and the narrowly defined interests of their particular constituencies rapidly become *displaced persons*. This, as I know, from being for a brief while engaged in a group which persuaded various persons from different positions (management, trade unions, local government and so on) to start considering their situation as human beings and in relation to the community, produces real pressure and real suffering.

For people are expected to conform to their constituency and their group, and the raising of these wider and deeper questions is resented by those they represent or to whom they have to report back. There is therefore real suffering in this which is probably not unrelated to the way in which Jesus

32

himself was a displaced person in the interests of newness and the kingdom of God. A carefully developed sustaining ministry in this area is therefore of the utmost importance in relation to the work of industrial mission on behalf of industry and society at large.

Fifthly and finally, industrial mission needs to develop, and become more efficient at, a compassionate and committed gadfly ministry to the churches. The churches need to be told that they have to wake up. Industry is not a specialized interest and a mere part of our society. It is a general interest and absolutely vital to, as well as influential in, our society as a whole. Industry, therefore, is both an essential promise and an inescapable threat as far as our society is concerned. It should not therefore be a side-issue in the life of the church and in Christian discipleship, but a central issue with regard to the ordinary life, concerns and ministries of the churches. Therefore industrial mission has a special responsibility to organize itself to say to the church 'Pay attention'.

For if God is God, and we pay attention, then he can and will give us ways through our confusions about industry and our confusions in industry which will lead us on to more human and creative ways of relating industry and society. It is in this context that I believe we should see both the challenge of Industry Year and also the opportunities of industrial mission. In a splendid letter published in *The Times* on 1 March 1986 entitled 'Keeping Balance on Sunday Trading', Cardinal Hume wrote:

For all its shortcomings, the regulated Sunday is a sign which points society beyond itself and affords people the opportunity of standing back, of renewing themselves. That is the meaning of 'recreation', without which human beings are not truly human – they are drudges.

We must beware lest the principle prevail that the Market

should rule supreme seven days a week. Our principle is that there is more to being human than simple supply and demand; there is more to social life than trading and commerce.

I have indicated only the beginnings of this important argument. But surely it is clear that we have enough grounds on the basis of the facts of what is going on, on the basis of what is happening to human beings and on the basis of faith, to insist that we are all challenged afresh both to discover what necessities are indeed pointed to by 'the Market', what limits are imposed by these necessities and in the way we respond to these necessities, and to discover new and creative ways of growing a new society with hope through the very difficult future which lies ahead of us.

4

The City of London, 1987

Lessons: Deuteronomy 26. 1–11
Hebrews 11. 1–4, 8–16

The job of the preacher in this service must be to suggest some possible interaction between a faith in the living God of the Bible, in whose name we are holding the service, the standing and affairs of the City of London, and the prospects for this New Year of 1987. The starting point for a preacher is something he or she believes is to be known about God. Hence my choice of readings from the Bible for this service. These readings are typical of a major thrust in the biblical dynamic and pattern of what it means to believe in God. As the first reading makes clear, to believe in the God of the Bible is to receive life as a gift and therefore as a responsibility. You may start as 'a wandering and homeless Aramaean', a tribal family wandering from one water-hole to the next, getting such a livelihood as you may in a world which is an uncertain wilderness. But to discover God, which is much more like being discovered by God, is to discover that the world is somehow or other transfused with a Power and a Possibility who intends purpose, direction and promise for those whom he calls to know him. So the very land you inhabit and the fruits and the profits which you reap there are to be seen as gifts. They are gifts given you for the purpose of collaborating with the God who encounters you and your people, cares for you, corrects you and keeps you seeking after a still richer and more obedient life of community and worship. To see, under God, that life and land, that first-fruits and profits, are gifts is to acknowledge one's dependency for them and to be called to face up to one's responsibility in the shared use of them.

The second reading makes it clear that this belief in, and experience of, God penetrates to the ultimate depths of reality and extends to the ultimate ranges of the future. 'By faith we perceive that the universe was fashioned by the word of God' (Hebrews 11.3). The activity and concern of the God who offers us our land, our labours and our first-fruits are the activity and concern of the Presence and Possibility responsible for all prescences and possibilities. God is not an option, still less is he a fiction. He may choose, for his mysterious purposes of creative sharing in love and freedom, to seek his purposes in ways of hiddenness, suffering and searching. For us who are Christians Jesus is the never fully understood but always sufficiently provocative evidence of this. But however hidden God is, he is there, the ultimately reality of all things and therefore the future certainty of all things.

So faith is not a religious relaxation from the pressures of reality for the spiritually minded. Nor is it a religious manipulation of realities for the superstitiously inclined. Faith is a glimpse both of what is offered to us and of what we are up against. We are offered collaboration, through the use of our land, the communities of our lives and the development of our labour, with an all-pervading presence of love and righteousness. We are up against an ultimate reality and a persistent and pressing future who will not be content with an abuse of matter, of possibilities and of people which turns them aside from being long-term opportunities and communities for creativity and sharing into short-term occasions for consumption, conflict and waste. God is always concerned with the future – a future which is more consistent with his love, more coherent with his holiness and more controlled by his reality. So men and women of faith are called to accept this responsibility from God and to seek this future of God which is both offered to them and demanded from them. 'That is why God is not ashamed to be called their God, for he has a city ready for them' (Hebrews 11. 16).

If we in any way share, or seek to share, in such a God, what interaction might there be between believing in a God like this, the affairs of the City of London and the prospects for 1987? Here, in the exercise of my responsibility as preacher, I have to select what steps I should take in seeking links between a working picture of God and the workings of the City of London in 1987. In selecting the steps I am about to describe I have, I believe, exercised my selective perception in a way which is consistent with biblical patterns of God's activity and purpose. Those who, in the Bible, seek to discern what God is saying to them, or what God would have them say to others, are portrayed as gaining insights into his counsels and purposes through what is happening to them and to the people to whom they belong. Current events and experiences interact with traditions and experiences of faith and worship to bring about new insights and demands together with renewal of old images and offers. So the living God of the tradition is found to be very much alive in the here and now and still to be pressing for his purposes and his future. In seeking to discharge my responsibility before God and before you in this service I have found two factors focussing my reflection.

First, as a bishop in the Church of England I receive both my salary and my working expenses directly from the Church Commissioners. This means that I am dependent both for the means by which I support my family and for the means by which I pursue my job on income raised from investments and from activities in the financial markets. Secondly, I am aware that now that this country imports more manufactured goods than it exports, we pay our way at the moment by invisible exports, tourism and the financial services industry which, I understand, in 1985 earned some £8 billion. This means that both in my particular personal post and as a citizen of the United Kingdom I have a direct awareness of, and a direct stake in, the activities of the City of London which are central to such prosperity and prospects as we at present have.

What, then, of the prospects for 1987? Surely, if one's faith in God gives some freedom and detachment from the taken-for-granted assumptions on which one is bound to conduct most of one's regular daily business most of the time, then we can see that the prospects are very uncertain indeed. All the major markets of the world, and the programmes and policies designed to support and promote them, are striving for growth related to material production and consumption. But this is almost certainly not sustainable and increasingly certainly not desirable. An overall growth of three per cent per annum, for example, would double production in twenty-five years, with a corresponding use of resources. And we have already nearly wrecked our limited planet. Also, competitive growth proceeds by capturing markets and rendering those already in the markets obsolescent. The system, therefore, is inherently un-stable and leaves a trail of losers who are an increasing burden and a threat. This is already well visible with the growth in the number of the unemployed in developed countries and the increasing poverty in undeveloped countries. It looks as if we have practically used up the possibilities of industrial capitalism over the past two hundred years or so and we now must invent something else if we are to survive and flourish.

The same instability and threat looks as if it is around in that set of activities with which the City of London is particularly associated, that is in the whole world of credit. Now that the so-called 'financial services industry' is globalized and computerized, it is probable that our current financial and ideological bluffs are on the verge of being sharply and decisively called. For instance, what is the effective connection between profit making transactions in the financial services market and industrial investment which will actually increase real wealth available through real communities for increasing numbers of actual human beings? How long can credit, which is secured (if at all) in other credit-making and credit-taking operations, actually be sustained? Especially if and when Third-World indebtedness at interest rates which absorb substanial proportions of their country's gross national products oblige Third World countries to 'default' – that is, declare that they are no longer going to play a game all of whose rules are set up so that they are bound to lose. And how will a twenty-four hour system of responses to market variations, which is programmed to respond to its own responses, avoid catastrophic over-reactions – let alone maintain any connection with creative and constructive human and social realities?

Finally, in considering the prospects for 1987, we have to ask whose prospects we are considering and how long-term prospects they are. Morality and community apart, it is doubtful if we can prudentially afford to neglect the prospects of the thirty per cent or more of the population of the United Kingdom who have no chance in the forseeable future of taking part in the prosperity produced by our market systems, even if those systems prove sustainable. In very large areas of Africa, Asia and Latin America those without prospects form far more than thirty per cent of the human mass. We have to consider whether we can expect them to be kept under control and the costs to the system of providing such control. To return to the actual operations of the present system, there is much to worry about in the short-term nature of the profitability of companies and enterprises which weighs heavily with the accountants and analysts who seem more and more to influence transactions in the financial services industry. Who, under current criteria and pressures, whether in the world of government or of finance, are ready to invest necessarily risked capital in the long-term and increasingly unforseeable future?

Prospects for 1987 and beyond therefore show very definite signs of high instability, uncertain sustainability and doubtful morality. Yet, as I have already said, the activities of the City of London are central to such prosperity as we at present have. We are all, therefore, challenged, put to the test, called in question. It is a questioning which transcends any politics, while it relativizes and disturbs all politics. It is the sort of fundamental questioning which those of us who have any sort of faith in the God of the Bible, or any sympathy with the moral and dynamic thrust of the Bible, might recognize as the pressure of God's future upon us. Here we encounter an expression of the reality in the structuring of our common being as human beings which is experienced in the receiving of life and resources as gifts and therefore as responsibilities. God is calling us in question because we are heading for a future which is either no future at all or else a future of increasing misery and threat for increasing numbers of our fellow human beings.

If this presentation and interpretation have any truth and reality in them, then there is a great deal of medium-term and long-term hope in the immediate uncertainties and threats. For God calls in question people – individuals, groups, communities and nations – not in order to confuse and destroy them but in order to redirect and renew them. If the industrial age dominated and motivated by sheer economic growth and sheer increase of material consumption is proving increasingly impracticable and nonsensical, then we have the chance of both discovering and inventing new ways of life together. These are

40

ways of life which are partly round the corner but probably partly already emerging among us.

The immediate question of 1987 is therefore how to live under God with a system which is running down, may blow up or collapse inwards, but is not yet replaceable. In the City of London this would seem to require at least the following. First, live with the wider realities. Do not allow yourself to be trapped into believing that, or behaving as if, your criteria and interests, still less what you can get on your computers or read on your computer screens, define or delimit what is going on, what can go on or what ought to go on. There is much more to humanity than that. And if God is God then there is very much more again.

Secondly, strengthen the responsibility and the mutual accountability with which you do the activities and tasks you at present do. This presumably means pressing on with the troublesome matters of structures of self-regulation and more public accountability with which you are already so busy.

Thirdly, remember charity and beware of greed. No doubt our society needs deep changes in the way it seeks justice and promotes mutual support. At the moment we are not at all clear in what direction to seek them; meanwhile – and under all conditions of society – direct personal morality is an essential part of faith in God, sharing with the neighbour and keeping open to the wider and deeper changes which society and the future require. If you prosper, then share your prosperity. And if morally and socially outrageous salaries are commanded by some or held to be required by the system, then consider whether this is not one more symptom of a system which is becoming morally decadent and prudentially unsustainable.

And, finally, build into your corporate planning and thinking an awareness of the need for constructive repentance, a rethinking which builds towards a more feasible future. We are going to have to build new forms of society, from the economic to the social. We cannot go on indefinitely as we are. The City ought to be as well equipped as any of our institutions to receive messages of a changing world and to contribute to such a society's search for a changed world.

Under God uncertain prospects can lead to constructive change; and with God uncomfortable personal questions can lead to new vision, new neighbourliness and new hope.

PART TWO

Faith in the City

5

Christian Doctrine: The Challenge to and from Poverty

The brief that I have been given is to draw your attention to some of the features of the traditional Christian story about God, men and women, and the world, which seem to me as a theologian to be particularly relevant to the challenge of poverty. As a theologian it is my job and my duty to point to what seem to me to be relevant factors or features in the tradition. I have to do this because I hold, on mature reflection, that these are features which Christians ought to take into account as they face up to and grapple with that experience of millions of people in the world that can be called 'poverty'.

I must make it quite clear that my comments are very deliberately put forward as material for the common task of working out the responsible and appropriate Christian actions in the face of this challenge. This task, like others, has to be undertaken by us as Christian citizens, and as Christian leaders and ministers. Here we all have to take theology into account, but I am increasingly clear that theologians as such do not have any privileged access to decisions about the nature and details of the task.

The task is quite clearly a common Christian responsibility. My job is to make a significant contribution to that task, *qua* theologian; it is not my job to define the task or delimit the task. I am making a contribution to what we all have to work out together.

What then, are some features of the traditional Christian story about God, men and women, and the world which are particularly relevant to the challenge of poverty?

First Christianity is not a this-worldly religion. It is the most this-worldly of other-worldly religions. I think it is absolutely vital to be clear about this, because there is much confusion at the moment, as there is at regular intervals, because many people cease to find the transcendent aspect of Christianity believable. But they attempt to strengthen the case of what they want to keep from Christianity by claiming that really Christianity must now be reduced to what it is they want to keep. I can give you two examples. The first is that quite a few people wish to go on being, in one way or another, Jesus admirers. But they cannot do with God, the Father of Jesus. Now Jesus admirers are not as such, Christians. Another example is people who hold that the Christian tradition either originated or very powerfully developed insights into freedom, justice and love. This they wish to keep, but again, not God. Now I think it is very important to be clear, especially with regard to practical actions and movements, that atheism is a very powerful and ever-present possibility. It may very well be that Christianity is unbelievable and that Christian faith is a stupid or tragic mistake. But it is also very important to be clear what follows from such a conclusion or decision.

Thus, any view one holds about one's favourite features of Jesus being somehow of general or universal significance becomes entirely subjective and, probably, entirely individual-istic once one has decided on atheism and rejected Christian faith in God. One's views become exceedingly difficult to dis-tinguish from wishful thinking. 'Jesus is the man for others', or 'Jesus means freedom', and so on, become subjective slogans.

Secondly, any claim that one might make about freedom and justice, and indeed love, having been somehow or other programmed into processes in nature or history, or somehow derivable from processes in nature and history, is likewise purely subjective. Such claims become exceedingly difficult to distinguish from whistling in the dark. Of course, if you are in a Sartrean dark you might as well whistle. This is a perfectly proper and possible position. But you cannot have the dynamic and hope of the Christian story without the God of the Christian story. It is very important doctrinally to be clear about the distinction between the 'truths of Christianity' and whether Christianity is true. You must distinguish the two. That is to say, Christianity does have a tradition and an impact and a direction, and a certain coherence. And you cannot dismantle it into bits. But you may still decide, being quite clear about the coherence and what you must believe if you are a Christian, that you cannot so believe. And if you cannot, you must not. There is the question about what you must believe as a Christian, then there is the question whether you can believe, and then there is the question whether you do believe it. And they should not be confused. And you cannot cook the 'must' in order to get away with the 'can'. All you then get is a can of worms.

I think this is absolutely clear. It is absolutely clear on historical grounds – the development of Christianity, the documents of Christianity and so on. They are just so riddled with God that if you cannot believe in God then you cannot be a Christian. It is also very clear on logical grounds, the way the language works. For example, great men like Tillich tried to get away with it by turning verbs with subjects into passive verbs. He proposed a phrase like 'I am accepted'. We thus avoid talk about God. But for language like 'I am accepted' to work there must be an agent who would come after the 'by' that he has left out. People are always playing this linguistic game and it is logically not on. It is also very clear that it will not do on practical grounds, because of course, one of the fundamental practical issues is about the resources around, the possibilities that are open, the place that they might be, and the salvation that might happen. And this matter seems to me to be of particular importance with regard to Christian doctrine, and the challenge of poverty.

This is because on the one hand it has been clear for years that poverty is a great area for bourgeois confusion and general romanticism. And so it is very easy to give it a sort of general social or religious veneer and start pottering about. But in view of the absolutely hellish nature of the problem, it is very important to be as clear as possible about what might be called the likely parameters of reality. What is around? Not only immediately, but ultimately? And what are the likely connections between what is around immediately and what might be around ultimately? But further, there is a very strong theological reason for raising this right at the beginning. This is that the existence and treatment of the poor is clearly a challenge to the Christian understanding of God. He is said to be loving, serving, acting and so on, so what the hell is he up to?

On the other hand it is also clear that the existence of poverty is challenged by any biblical and Christian understanding of God. Thus my first doctrinal point is that Christianity is (as a matter of fact like all religions) an other-worldly religion. That is to say, the story it tells and lives by concerning men and women in the world allocates a principal and necessary part to God; and God is other-worldly. He goes beyond and exists beyond the resources and facts of this world as a transcendent resource and fact for the world, and as offering a fulfilment to men and women who are in the world which comes from beyond the world and goes beyond the world.

The second relevant doctrinal point is a development of the

point about the most worldly, the most this-worldly of other-worldly religions. Start from the obvious point. For Christians, the true story about God, men and women, and the world is focussed by and embodied in Jesus. Christianity started because Jesus was identified as the Christ. And Christianity continued because Jesus identified as the Christ became clearly understood, clearly believed in and clearly followed as Jesus Christ our Lord – the Christ of God who is, in fact, God's Vice-Regent, our Lord, the way in which the Lord comes to us. And so Christians are soon talking about the grace of our Lord Jesus Christ, the love of God and the fellowship of the Holy Spirit all in one breath, which produced what is perhaps the distinctive symbol of Christian insight into and Christian claims about God, the Holy Trinity. That is to say, as God is in himself, so he is in the flesh and blood of Jesus, and so he is in the continuing presence and work of the Holy Spirit. Now, this belief, this story, this claim, this insight of faith, engages and enmeshes together the transcendent and the other-worldly God in this-worldly particularities and events in an absolutely unique way, and in a quite extraordinarily challenging way. Transcendence, particularity, immanent and continuing working, are all engaged together. But none of them is reduced to another.

This is an unexpected fulfilment and a remarkable transformation of a very strong strand in the understanding of, and the story about, God which has grown up through the work of the prophets and which is in fact present in all Old Testament writing, not least in the Psalms. It is a strand about the understanding of God which is absolutely crucial with regard to the matter of poverty. This is the steadily deepening and unshakeable conviction that somehow or other there is a moral power and a moral possibility buried deep in, and at work in, the often savage randomness of human affairs. Read the prophets and you will find that they like the psalmists, have an extra-ordinary capacity to perceive, to hang on to and to live by evidence that in the midst of both natural phenomena and historical achievements and catastrophes it is possible to serve and respond to the Lord. From Jeremiah we read page after page, now collected together, of gloom and doom. But in it there is the Lord. There are splendid psalms that talk about 'the sea raging mightily', the heavens doing this and that, and the sun running about the place, and then you come to the Lord, and then you come to the Law, and then you come to the people. It is all of a piece. The Lord has chosen Israel to know him and name him and to serve him. And it is eventually discovered that as he is the God of the earth and heavens, his purpose in and through Israel is a purpose for the whole earth and whole heavens. That eventually develops. But long before this is what you might call clear 'doctrinally', the point is made again and again that the Lord is the ultimate over-riding power of all that is and of all that happens, and that his concerns are holy and righteous. Hence, through all the ups and downs of the life and religion of Israel and Judah there develops a great longing, a longing which is of the utmost importance humanly. This is a longing for the establishment of God's holiness, of his covenant love, of his righteousness and of his peace. The longing and the hope is that this will be established through a people who are transformed into a people of holiness, love, righteousness and peace. The whole thing is informed and transformed again and again by a passion for the fruits of righteousness and peace in a holy community and a holy society. Along with this recognition of the holy and righteous Lord, and as part of this longing for righteousness, love and peace, there is a matching anger and outrage against all the deceitful and distorting ways of man. It is of the utmost importance to be clear that this anger and outrage is not just fed-upness, is not just frustration, and is not just the anger of the underdog. That anger, arising from being constantly trampled upon, is anger enough. But this is something much deeper, more blinding and more burning, and therefore ultimately more hopeful. It is the anger and the outrage which goes with the longing for holiness and righteousness. It is part of the recognition and the worship of the Lord as a holy and transcendent God.

And so the effects of the recognition and the worship is, according to the prophets, a longing for righteousness and peace in the society of Israel and in the whole world, and as an absolutely integral part of the worship and the hope there is this outrage at the actual conditions of society which are an offence to the holiness, righteousness, love and peace of God.

Now as we all know very well, the sharpest focus (or rather the sharpest foci) for this anger, which is the other side of longing, is twofold: idolatry and the treatment of the poor. Idolatry is manifested by many ways of commitment to the piling up of wealth, and the irresponsible enjoyment of luxury. For self-indulgence and sensuousness are forms of idolatry. This is what 'you put your money on', and you have gods that you can carry about so that you can fix them. The other side is the treatment of the poor. References to this are easily to be found. Repetition, I fear, can dull them, but the impact is absolutely clear, and I thought that just to remind you I would select verses from the first ten chapters of Isaiah.

First of all (from a passage which starts with 'Your country being desolate ...'):

Cease to do evil and learn to do right
Pursue justice and champion the oppressed
Give the orphan his rights
Plead the widow's cause.

And then later:

51

How the faithful city has played the whore.
Once the home of justice where righteousness dwelt
Now murderers.
Your silver has turned into base metal
And your liquor is diluted with water.
Your very rulers are rebels
Confederate with thieves.
Every man of them loves a bribe and itches for a gift.
They do not give the orphan his rights
And the widow's cause never comes before them.

And so it goes on. Then there is Chapter 5 about 'My beloved concerning a vineyard', with:

Shame on you, you who add house to house
And join field to field
Until not an acre remains
And you are left to dwell alone in the land (v.8).

Or Chapter 10, at the beginning:

Shame on you, you who make unjust laws and
publish burdensome decrees,
Depriving the poor of justice,
Robbing the weakest of my people of their rights,
Despoiling the widow and plundering the orphan.
What will you do when called to account,
When ruin from afar confronts you?

The story which Christianity takes up is the story of the righteous and saving God who is at the heart of all things, as part of his being beyond all things. We have to do with this most this-worldly of other-worldly religions, and the focus of the transcendent involvement in this world is holiness and righteousness: holiness and righteousness, that is, which brings under judgment all that is contrary to love and peace. And a major focus of all this is anger against the idolatry of wealth and the treatment of the poor.

Now we move to the next point in my theological attempt to draw your attention to doctrines relevant to the challenge of poverty. We are Christians, as I have already pointed out, because we belong to those who believe that Jesus focusses and defines God's commitment to this story of the righteous and saving God. The life, the death and the resurrection of Jesus means that this story is both vindicated and promised an end. Vindication is offered because the holy and righteous God, whose concern is love and peace, gives us himself in the flesh and blood of his Son, right in the midst, precisely as part of the world in all its goings-on and gettings-down, utterly and humanly down to earth. This may seem quite unbelievable, but 'there's glory for you' – this is really what it is about. It is also deeply disturbing, because here is a possibility of holiness for you, right in the midst. Nothing could be more this-worldly, and this Jesus is declared by the resurrection and by the coming of the Spirit to be the sign, the word of the transcendent God. This is put into its transcendent context by talking about his being seated at the right hand of God and coming again to judge the quick and the dead. So the story is not only vindicated but its hope of an end is also underwritten. So there is the promise of an end. Holiness and righteousness will, in the end, establish love and peace.

But now we come to what may well be the most difficult and possibly the most controversial part of what I want to say. I think, however, that it is critical, and it is the best I can do. That is to say: this is where my theological investigation has so far brought me. Let me try to give you the argument and then finish up by saying how it seems to me to bear on the poor. There is a promised end to the story. And as the story is vindicated as true, the promised end will truly come. The question is, where and how? The doctrinal answer, as far as I can see it, is this. The answer to the question where and how, is and always is, *not yet*. As far as we are concerned, there is no getting beyond this. Consider. In the days of the flesh of Jesus, the expectation seemed to be pretty clear, 'the end is at hand'. One of the reasons why the groups described early in the Acts of the Apostles thought that they could live like communists was that they felt that they had only a few weeks or months to live. But they had to live longer than that and the communism did not last. After the resurrection of Jesus and the coming of the Spirit followed what in technical terms is called 'the delay of the parousia'. That is to say, the Lord did not return or, if that is not the right way of putting it, God did not make an end.

Now this matter of what comes to be called 'a delay in the parousia', the apparent falsification of an expectation of 'the end is at hand', is not to be interpreted either as a mistake or as an indefinite prolongation. That is to say, one cannot get out of this dilemma of the New Testament evidence and the struggles of the early church on the one hand by saying: 'Well, it was a mistake but it wasn't a mistake of substance. After all, what we're really dealing with is that there is nothing but a heavenly kingdom.' Block out the notion of there being an end, and of there being a working towards this and all the rest of it. Be quite clear, with the help of the Greeks, who after all have done quite a lot to help us, that the end isn't the end of time or the end in time; it's 'up there'. Eternity is what we are talking about. And the following of Jesus Christ is the business of getting in the right mood and mode for eternity. That move into nothing but eternity is, I believe, a mistake. It does not do justice to the force of the language and the dynamism of the expectations Jesus both arranged and fulfilled. Nor is it right simply to reinterpret in terms of an indefinite prolongation. That reinterpretation starts very explicitly in II Peter 3.8: 'You may be bothered that the Lord has not come back, but you must remember that with the Lord, a thousand years is as one day, so you have not had a week yet.' This is absolutely brilliant stuff, but you cannot get away with such reinterpretation indefinitely.

The notion that the coming of the End is indefinitely prolonged, but that it may be that the earthly kingdom will happen tomorrow or the next day or if we can only get round the next corner, is in fact as mistaken as the business of shoving the kingdom into nothing but eternity. We have to receive this whole matter as the structuring of how we are to live by the faith of this most this-worldly of other-worldly religions. It is the structuring of a dynamic truth and tension. Responding through Jesus Christ and in the Spirit to the transcendent God of holiness and righteousness, who promises love and peace in the end, requires us to live and gives us the glorious chance to live 'eschatologically'. Eschatological living is structured in a three-dimensional way. You have to live under the judgment of the kingdom which is at hand. Therefore you are constantly called, even if you have to tolerate the intolerable, not to pretend it is tolerable. The judgment is straight down from above, always in the here and now, about the kingdom which is at hand. And it is intolerable to the power and presence and possibility of the kingdom that these sorts of things should be going on. You have to live, secondly, as part of building the kingdom which is in the midst (I will come to unpack each of these in a minute.) So, under the judgment of the kingdom which is at hand we are to be part of building the kingdom which is in the midst. And, thirdly, we are waiting for the coming of the kingdom which is promised.

Anything less than an attempt to have one's life, practices and plans structured by these threefold shaping forces spoils the story and fails to cope with the realities we have to face. The Christian story is spoilt, for example, by a complete other-worldliness which is foreign to it and hopelessly narrows its claim. On the other hand, deny transcendence and secularize everything and you move into non-successful this-worldliness. You keep on producing an arrested development *en route* (it is supposed) for this-worldly utopia, and politics and government become new forms, either of tyranny or waiting for Godot. Further, if you simply juggle with all this and are sometimes vaguely other-worldly, you produce what you might call an ordinary religiosity which has the disadvantage of being neither here nor there. Such religiosity does not really engage with this world nor take you up into the heights of transcendence; so what is the good of it?

Anything less than this threefold eschatological structure not only spoils the story; it also fails to cope with reality. One is unable to engage the realities of God in his transcendence and his coming and the realities of history, which do not build up steadily in some guaranteed direction but keep on having the most amazing opportunities as well as the most dreadful threats and failures. Nor can one engage with the realities of the personal and ordinary here and now where people are suffering, where they need hope, and where they need evidence of caring, where they need a foretaste of the kingdom and so on. Our hopeful story and our experienced realities will fall apart unless we understand that we are offered or (in a rather less exalted mood) threatened with this threefold interaction of what I have called judgment, building and waiting. This can be related to the heart of Christian doctrine through a sentence which is a summary of the story from the doctrinal point of view: 'God is as he is in Jesus, so there is hope.' God is transcendent other-worldliness, power from beyond, promise of an end. But this God is as he is in Jesus, utterly involved in and committed to this-worldliness – of course, at a cost. So there is hope. The question is, how to live under the pressure and promise of this hope. The answer seems to me to be (and this is where we come finally to poverty) by this-worldly commitment worked out and worked at in the Christian three-dimensional way – being judged, being part of building, and waiting.

Now if you combine a responsible study of the biblical material for the story with a responsible analysis of the present pressures on and in our society, I think you will see just how vital and central is the issue of poverty and the poor: central, that is, to the issue of the this-worldly commitment demanded by our other-worldly Christian religion. First, we have the judgment of the kingdom which is at hand. What offends righteousness and justice, as it is longed for and related to God in the Old Testament, more than the exclusion of an increasing number of persons from society both in its basis and in its power? What is more contrary to love than steadily adding to the number of people whom one will not recognize as one's neighbour? What threatens peace more than a steady building up of numbers of persons who have no hope, no belonging and no status? It is not so much poverty understood as an absolute low level or a particular standard of living, but the condition of the poor as excluded from a society which is off after false gods, and of the poor as exploited by society for false and destructive ends. Of course, material standards of living are relevant with regard to the poor – both with regard to a floor of minimum provision, and with regard to standards of comparison. But the issue is not fundamentally a quantitative one. This is important if we are going to avoid being constantly side-tracked by people who say 'Ah, but . . .there isn't going to be enough money' or 'Ah, but . . . we are no longer in a period of expansion, but in the period of retrenchment' and conclude that nothing can be done. The issue is not fundamentally quantitative, though of course people are particularly vulnerable because of shortage of resources. The fundamental issue is the exclusion from society which is itself going after false gods, and the exploitation by society for false and destructive ends.

And as the prophets knew perfectly well, socieities run like this cannot last. They cannot develop creatively and, what is more, they cannot survive external crises. That is a point that the prophets seemed to be making again and again.

Secondly, we come to the building of the kingdom which is in the midst. Here we are confronted by the sheer force of the question, 'And who is my neighbour'? Who are the people whom society has left by the wayside with their urgent needs neglected, as in the parable of the Good Samaritan? Surely the poor are neighbours who require the same sign from us of the caring of the kingdom? The response to this must be persistent attempts to 'realize' the situation: that is, to make it real so that ourselves and other people realize it. This must be done not in anger, but in analysis, as a steady facing-up to the facts of the case. And then there must be a working out persistent ways of offering some recognition to the poor, recognition as human beings, recognition as citizens, recognition as neighbours. That involves finding ways and means to offer something promising, not to offer the moon, not to offer prosperity now, not to offer some utopian picture which everybody knows cannot come, but something which you might call in biblical terms a substantial down-payment, a real earnest and foretaste of recognition of belonging, of neighbourliness. We have to be part of promoting political policies that give some real promise that there will be a development of sharing.

Finally, we come to waiting for the coming of the kingdom which is promised. This is absolutely vital if we are not to be put off by the impossibilities, the failures and the threats. I recently came across a remarkable verse in Jeremiah, Jeremiah 18.12:

But they answer, things are past hope.
We will do as we like,
And each of us will follow the promptings
   of his own wicked and stubborn heart.

58

This is a remarkable characterization of much in our society at the moment. There is no real hope, so let them stew in their own juice and we will do as nicely as we can. But according to the Christian story, things are never past hope. There is hope in being under judgment, there is hope through building, and there is hope in the light of the promise. But of course if one does not face up to all this with the intention of working out practical responses, then it is all threat. Yet the effect of the Christian understanding of the 'not yet' of the kingdom and the final end is to keep the story open, with space for us to repent, respond and reconstruct, and to do it in detailed and piecemeal ways. We do not have to produce the blueprint. That is part of the openness of the promise. 'Not yet' does not mean 'so it is hopeless'. It means: until the end it is hopeful. As far as we are concerned, our part in history may end with apocalypse. It will certainly end with our own deaths. But until this end we live in hope. For example, there has been progress and now it's a question of not going back on it. Thus, a whole lot of discussions on the welfare state seems to me to be hopeless in quite the wrong way. Of course a lot of it has not worked. Has anything ever worked as we meant it to? But there must be no going back on that which was good and that which was achieved. Progress does not go smoothly, just like that. It hiccups up and down, is a creation and an achievement which can be lost. We must fight like hell to prevent our going back on what has thus far been achieved. Again, improvements in a piecemeal way are absolutely vital, and simply because all sorts of things cannot be done there is no excuse whatever for not doing what can be done. What have to be tackled are the most pressing evils, where they are most pressing. We do not have to be bothering too much about constructing the overall good; that is God's job. It is he who offers openness and an overall community until the end.

My doctrinal investigations therefore suggest the following

working conclusions. We have the urgent opportunity to take seriously the Christian story about God, men and women and the world, with its twofoldness of the transcendent other-worldly God who is committed in righteousness and holiness to this world, for the purposes of love and peace. Consequently, we live under the threefold eschatological structure of the judgment of the kingdom, the building of the kingdom, and waiting for the kingdom. And with regard to poverty, this makes absolutely clear certain things that we have to be clear about and make clear to other people. First, poverty is morally offensive as well as divinely offensive. It is really troubling. It is not one of the unfortunate incidents on the way until we get somewhere. Secondly, poverty is in fact morally, humanly and divinely intolerable in its aspects of exclusion and exploitation. So it is not only really troubling, it is really urgent. And thirdly, poverty is socially destructive. And so it is practically and prudentially urgent to tackle it. And as William Temple and many others have pointed out, the way you have to move towards righteousness in political matters is to get at people prudentially. It is absolutely no good trying to promote a policy which would work only if most people were either saints or heroes or both. So we have to show how facing up to poverty is practically and prudentially urgent.

This means insisting that there must be no provisionality in recognizing and admitting the realities and demands of poverty and the poor. Of course there will have to be arguments and provisionality about the programmes that are required. But people must not be allowed to get away from the demands of recognition and from the troubling and urgent nature of the problem by saying this programme does not work or that programme does not work. Programmes are matters which always have to be discussed in detail, become provisional and have to be changed. But poverty is perpetually urgent, and therefore *poverty becomes a pressure of equal priority with everything else*. We must not wait to devise serious measures for dealing with poverty until some other measures (designed, for example, to increase production or deal with inflation) succeed. Because of pressures which combine theological, moral and prudential considerations we have to insist that facing up to poverty has as powerful a political priority as any other issue. The notion that you can delay responding to poverty is disastrous for our politics and our society. What can be done immediately is, of course, debatable, but it must involve recognition of the poor as neighbours and citizens and the developing of something promising for them. There must be concrete evidence and examples of such things – actual 'down-payments', as I said above.

Finally, this involves taking risks. Risks have, of course, to be properly calculated, but I would think of two areas immediately where risks need to be taken in relation to giving measures against poverty equal priority. These are risks with regard to inflation on the one hand, and to defence on the other. If we are taking poverty *equally* seriously, then we shall have to take risks and face uncertainties in the poverty area, but we must also take risks and face uncertainties in other areas. We must not excuse ourselves from tackling the poverty area in order to avoid risks or with the excuse of avoiding risks in other areas.

This pressure for equal priority arises because there is a very real sense in which these demands about the poor come 'from beyond'. They come from beyond any political stance, programme or ideology, and disturb and interfere with all such. They are rooted in our understanding of God. Of course much to do with the poor is totally dependent on so many other things. But poverty is also an independent issue. It does not depend on your theory about the market, or the community, or anything else. It comes from beyond in a basic understanding of God, men and women, and the world. Our situation is desperately urgent. And yet, the combination of urgency and desperation could combine to be hopeful and creative. For one of the features of the prophetic message and insight as reinforced in Jesus seems to me to be this. Apocalyptic pressures, if they are responded to by repentance and appropriate action, can be transmuted into the possibilities of hope. Can be but may not be. This is part of our freedom, and part of the space that God allows. The pressures on us are apocalyptic, but the story tells us and our faith tells us, that they can be transmuted into the possibilities of hope. As far as I can see, our faith in the God and Father of our Lord Jesus Christ who offers to work with us in and through the Spirit gives us absolutely no guarantee of earthly success on any front whatever. But what our faith does offer is the assurance and certainty that there is no such thing as total failure. The situation, until the end, is always open – and open always to creative and redeeming possibilities. So we are free always to work and always to hope, and to do this as practically as possible, and to do it as urgently as possible.

6

The Church, the Inner City and the Wilderness

This unfinished investigation is the beginning of exploring the following threefold thesis:

First, the inner city is now proving to be the most urgent symptom and symbol of the condition of our society.

Secondly, this condition is one of being lost in a wilderness of social incoherence, uncertainty and alienation. So that we need urgently to regain some common social momentum.

Thirdly, this provides a radical challenge to all our institutions, including the church: though I shall not say very much about this last part of the thesis, it is really what it points forward to.

The unfinished investigation moves somewhat like this. Consider the inner city as symptom and symbol. Pick up, for instance, the character of what have come to be called 'Urban Priority Areas'. These, in a number of more or less convergent definitions, are areas where a significant portion of the population suffers from deprivation in *two or more of at least five things*: unemployment, overcrowded housing, inadequate housing, single-parent families and single pensioners. The advantage of this sort of classification is that it does actually turn on statistics in the first place, so you are starting with what are undeniable 'hard facts' – probably 'hard facts' which are hard in more senses than one. The deprivations which are listed like this of course reinforce one another, and so we are faced with multiple-problem communities. Of course, these communities or the groups of persons who suffer these interlocking multiple deprivations are not confined to inner cities, as I have become very well aware as I move round the North East. There are other areas now called 'socially deprived' which are more outside the cities on the estates, some in my diocese where unemployment lies between thirty-five and eighty per cent and you get the usual spread of single-parent families and so on. There is plenty of deprivation and worry and despair as well. But surely there is a particular and peculiar concentration of our problems in the inner cities.

Moreover, and this is the next step in the argument, in the big inner cities problems are highlighted by the ethnic minorities. And they are doubtless further highlighted by the way in which inner cities attract crime. As soon as we start putting these factors together we at once become aware that there is liable to be a difference of opinion about what are the most important, shall we say, diagnostic symptoms. One of the things I want to argue is that the diagnostic symptoms that people choose can well be seen to be symbolic of the approach they are making to society as a whole. You highlight one cause or another because you have a certain picture which you may take for granted or which may be imposed by your ideology or by other presuppositions about what you think life is really like. Anyway, in these areas of multiple deprivation, whether you find them in an inner city – especially in some of the biggest cities – or not, you get an ethnic minority, crime and therefore a most explosive mix, producing, as we very well know, riots. What the riots bring out, I believe, is that it is here in the inner cities that we see sharply and quite inescapably how much we are in danger in our society of becoming two nations, the haves and the have-nots in a broad sense. Here we see the real threats of this and the difficult questions which are thereby faced. One of the things I want to consider is the way in which it seems to me most of us, most of the time, want really to dodge the real questions which are raised by what is going on and what is likely to go on, in our inner cities.

This matter of being or becoming two nations is of course not just a North–South divide, but more to do with those who are deprived and those who are in situations which reinforce their deprivation over against those who have opportunities and still have a chance to take off. Though it is clear that there is a strong tendency for the two nations to tend to fall, as it were, North, North-Westwards and North-Eastwards, over against things which tend to be South-East and South-West, with much of the Midlands increasingly becoming so to speak, 'beyond the pale'. Until, at any rate, very recently, these tendencies have been accelerated by the distribution of unemployment. It may be that we have now at last reached a plateau, but even so there is still the very grave problem with which we are faced that there are now whole areas of people, some of them in inner cities, some of them elsewhere, who are plainly more and more excluded by the conditions under which they live from our society or marginalized by it. This seems to me to be of particular significance at the present time because the main thrust which is offered to us as a way of getting out of our problems is what you might I think not unfairly call 'the competitive one'. It seems to me clear that the whole business of competitive take-off simply cannot occur in these multiple deprived areas. We seem to be confronted in this country with a revival of something which we used to argue about at great length in the World Council of Churches over development generally, which was known as the 'trickle-down theory'. If you can enable a competitive élite to make money and to multiply things rapidly you will then produce wealth which will trickle down to the rest. The general statistical evidence, at any rate over a considerable number of years, seems to have been that in what used to be called the under-developed countries the trickle-down theory does not work. This is clearly one of the most important challenges to us in our country at the present time.

So, whereas the whole problem of our society in its multiple deprivation, in the problems of unemployment and so on, is nothing like confined to the inner city, surely it is in the inner city that the mix is highly concentrated and for additional reasons becomes highly inflammable and therefore breaks out in a way to which people have to attend. And so the inner-city situation and inner-city happenings become highly diagnostic happenings. The way people respond to it becomes highly significant about the chances of our society and the way it will develop and so on. As one example of a sort of diagnostic comment I would like to quote at some length from a letter which appeared in *The Times* on 4 November 1986 from an American, Professor Bostet.

> Riots are the politics of the excluded. The current conventional wisdom about unemployment and the police does not go deeply enough to get at the sources of British inner-city riots. Until the communities from which riots spring have gained political recognition and representation riots will continue. The best evidence for this proposition is the American experience of the last twenty years.

And here he makes a very interesting historical comment:

> In eighteenth-century bread riots and nineteenth- and twentieth-centry industrial clashes and battles for the vote by the middle-class or working-class men and by women, rioters have used force as political leverage when they were excluded from the routine processes of power.

He then further expounds this, but we needn't go into it at great length. Then he adds the interesting point:

66

The police have been the triggers and targets of riot because they are the face of an alien power structure. Tragic police mistakes like those at Brixton and Tottenham are fortunately few, but they provoke ferocious black outrage in the context of one ethnic group policing another.

And he puts it pointedly: 'compare Northern Ireland'. Those who have a monopoly of power have a monopoly of responsibility. Then he goes on to say that the United States has by no means satisfied the aspirations of its black citizens, but they have produced leaders who are both a symbol of real hope and mobility and a real black presence in the power of the establishment. And he ends:

The real challenge for the British political system is to include black Britons as policy makers, not merely as the objects of policy. Can the centralized majoritarian party system accommodate minorities? Until it does, history suggests rioting will reoccur.

These seem to me to be very clear and suggestive comments which can be more widely applied. Just as it would be quite wrong, and could produce disastrous results, to make crime the main cause of the riots, so in fact it could be very misleading to make race the prime and only cause of the riots. Because they are in fact drawing attention to a condition which is highlighted in the inner cities and strengthened by the racial situation, which is that, more generally, there are vast areas of our country – and very considerable numbers of people in them – who have no share in our society, or practically none, and no hope of a share. This is thrown into high relief by an inner-city situation with a black minority, and especially a West Indian minority, because the blacks are the outsiders *par excellence* and they have an identity of their own, so they are liable to react more violently on this issue.

There was a significant comment in one of *The Economist*'s editorials on 12 October 1985, which was about the black's future, where this interesting remark was made:

> Black people with jobs do not riot in the streets. Nor do unemployed white people where the level of black discontent is absent – as in the cities of Northern England and Scotland – though they and the employed sometimes riot at football matches instead.

But look how that is put. 'Unemployed white people don't riot where the level of black discontent is absent.' That, I think, is a very diagnostic and give-away and significant remark. I myself have felt when moving round the North East that what is remarkable is that there is so little violence given the amount of unemployment, of shared nothing-to-do-ness and the number of youths, for instance, hanging around in city centres. And so what the inner city situation draws attention to, and draws attention to in a very sharp and particularly frightening way, is the significant existence of 'no go' areas.

The first point about the 'no go' areas is that nothing goes in them. There is nothing happening very much – it is amazing what is happening if you look into it, but nothing that can lead to hope of positive development. And for anyone born and brought up in these areas, there is nowhere to go. It is a 'no go' area indeed. It is a hopeless perversion of facing up to the realities of the human and political situation to say that the first thing about such an area is that it is a 'no go' area for the elderly and the police. That is true and has to be dealt with, and it has somehow to be handled, but to separate this from the other elements of a no go area seems to me to be quite disastrous.

We are being confronted in the inner cities with the evidence that we are really and dangerously becoming two nations which will become more and more opposed to one another.

Now, it may well be said, 'but what's new about all this?' Disraeli wrote a book about two nations long ago, and the whole of history indicates that societies have always fallen apart into those who have and manage to keep things under control and those who have not and struggle but don't get very far. Therefore, perhaps, apart from racial tension, our present situation is no different from the whole of history. So perhaps the question, when one is confronted with this very difficult situation, is not so much 'what's new about it' but 'what's different about it?'

Here I come to a thesis which has been forming in my mind and which I want to share with you because I think it is probably true. It has occurred to me lately, and I hope I can show that this is relevant to our general subject and our general concerns, that what is different about our present situation, the present conflicts between the haves and have-nots, and the dangers of the two nations, is actually *progress*. Progress is different, because things have progressed. Or rather the human project has, however, precariously and episodically, actually moved on. It is quite absurd, of course, to try now to establish support for this thesis, but I will attempt a brief indication of the arguments which can, I believe, be developed.

It is really a question of what has been happening from at least the American and French revolutions onwards. In various ways there has been a concern for, let us say, 'liberty, fraternity and equality'. This concern has been forced in to the fabric of societies, very often by the challenges of Marxism. Whereas there is undoubtedly something very ambivalent about Marxism, and idolatry of a total ideology is extremely dangerous, nonetheless Marxism has made many people realize the possibility of an alternative: there is no need to tolerate this total and constant division into two nations. We in this country experienced it, especially persons of my age, in the whole build-up towards the welfare state, which was considered –

although it was eventually based by Beveridge on insurance contributions and so on – as some really basic organized attempt by our society to care and to share burdens. We are also confronted now with the way in which in some real sense there is an increasing sense of one world. We have the business of the response to famine. We have the business of acute anxiety over apartheid. We have a lot of liberation talk, we have many peace movements, we have Green parties and so on. There has been progress over the last two hundred and fifty years also in the attempt for all human beings to take other human beings equally seriously and this has affected expectations of and attitudes towards human beings in society.

I cannot go into that further now, but the point about it is that I think it is extremely likely that the two nations business – the mere acceptance of their existence, the mere saying 'Well, it has always been like this and we have always had to struggle and we have also always had to deal with conflict', will in fact prove not to be acceptable. We cannot go back on things that we have begun to discover, however hard-earned our progress, however fragile our progress, however episodic – you go three forward and you slip two back in this area of liberty, fraternity and equality. But there *is* progress.

People may then respond, but that is really very wet and romantic; there are endless grounds for caution, scepticism, even cynicism about the way in which what we call progress simply does not come off. It looks as though there is a persistent failure to recognize the limits of human possibilities and the limits of human beings, the limits of human altruism and all the rest of it. And certainly what at any rate the Christians would call sin, is very rampant and around. Power often goes on being corrupted. You have a revolution and then it goes wrong and in any case, as many people might say at the moment, why trust any politicians anywhere ever? Further, there is perpetual evidence that we are faced with what the

Greeks called *'pleonexia'*, which is the human tendency always to want more. If you always want more, then this breaks down the discipline of any socialist society as well as any capitalist society and perhaps the only way to check the lavish use of resources and then the fact that you go bankrupt is by the policies of the market. Also, we are always confronted by bureaucracies and size. (So beware of the state. There is often ambivalence here – we are told that we should be afraid of collectivism and State intervention, because of bureaucracies and size, but we do not appear to have to be afraid of multi-national corporations because of bureaucracies and size. Which again suggests that what you take as being diagnostically symptomatic is symbolic of the way you are looking at things.)

Anyway, there are a number of arguments about why we should not resume any belief in progress or any belief that we can expect to move the human project forward. Many people seem to argue that the only hard realities are things like the super-power struggle, the competitive industrial struggle and the Market. This sort of thing gets very easily developed into what I would call 'practical atheism'. This leaves the issue of God and absolutes entirely out of consideration and does not notice that the effect is not to make everything reletavized and negotiable but rather to absolutize whatever system we are living by. We are confronted with this practical atheism of a down-to-earth and very dull and dreary sort in the way politics are handled at the moment. The most famous example of this is that faithless phrase 'better dead than red', which shows such a lack of faith in ourselves that one does not even get to the question of faith about God. Or another phrase which is around at the moment; 'There is no alternative.' Who told us there is no alternative? Or there is the way in which parties on the Left seem to prefer sectarian purity and righteousness to political effectiveness. Or a most remarkable blindness seems to be repeated again and again over the situation in South Africa.

To this day people in papers are producing the argument: 'No, we had better not have sanctions against South Africa because, after all, it is in the economy that the blacks will be more hurt than anywhere else.' But who do they think the blacks are? Do they not understand that – it is very odd, no doubt, and of course most upsetting – actually people get to the point where they care more about being recognized as persons than about any economies whatever? But there seems to be no awareness of this. It comes up in *The Times* regularly.

I suspect that there is a great danger of Mrs Thatcher's government acting in their own way as desperately as the rioters because they seem to be getting themselves into a corner in which, although their policy is not working, they are convinced it must work, so there must be more of the same at all costs. Hence the incredible short-sightedness and set of improvisations by people who are supposed to be making long-term investments in some sort of long-term future.

The point I have been making is that it is said again and again that there is nowhere else to turn, for it has all been tried and has failed. We have therefore to face the question, surely, whether we are right to concede or conclude that there is no human project and that there is no sense in which we can either believe in some progress achieved and start working to re-achieve some further progress. Is there no human project and are we going nowhere?

This has become very clear to me: that although you have to remain as realistic as you possibly can this is in fact a question of faith. I find myself on the spot because of my Christian faith. I am not claiming that people should share that; I am just trying to explain. Because of Jesus Christ I do not believe that we are to abandon a human project. I was reminded when writing this of Martin Luther King's 'I have a dream'. He had this dream because he had faith. We need to be reminded that the kingdom of God may remain a dream and a source of dreams, but it is not an illusion. Not, at any rate, if one is a Christian. It is the offer of God to all men and women, to all who have the potential to share in worth. That is to say: to be part of being, to be part of caring, to be part of sharing, to be taken up in justice and truth and love and joy and holiness and so on. Surely the Bible makes clear to us that we do not have to deal with a cultic god who is in a parochial way concerned with the faith and the future of a very selectively and exclusively chosen people. The Bible is about the great, glorious and mysterious God who has a project of love for all, who works those purposes through various groups of chosen people who again and again have to be disabused of the notion that God chose them especially for themselves. (I always think that if any congregation went home and looked in a mirror they would see that God must have some better reason than just choosing them!)

So Christians surely must be alert to the fact that they are called to believe in the possibility of this human project, this human project which God has apparently invested in with great risk in the whole matter of what we call 'creation'. So we must sustain the claim that what goes on in the world has purpose, a purpose which has been reinforced by what we call redemption. Sufficient signs have been offered, and in Jesus Christ compelling signs, that God is at work to identify with, suffer and redeem his project.

Therefore we may not say that there is no human project. We must be clear that people have great worth and that progress has been possible in striving for this worth and that progress may be resumed in the pursuit of this worth. And lest you should feel that this is too theological and too romantic (because faith never gets down-to-earth) I would point out that this ties up with what I might call prudential fact. People *have* been awakened, right across the world, and in history, to their rights and their values. They are not likely to give up and forget this and go back to being what you might call passive peasant fodder or whatever it is. Further, I think that this fact of faith and this fact of prudence ties up with what I might call a moral fact which has been well indicated by the response through the television appeals to Ethiopia and so on. People actually are moved by compassion. It is not always a question of some theory about human rights; it is a question about a basic feeling that human beings should be cared for. Suffering is as much a compulsion to do something as are rights, though of course in political situations you have to bring the two together. Hence we can be clear that we are not to give up a notion of progress in helping human beings to discover and share worth. Which returns us to the current conditions and circumstances of our society focussed in our inner cities.

The inner cities surely hold up a mirror to ourselves as a society. We have to ask ourselves whether we have given up the admittedly difficult and never to be fully achieved aim of progress as a caring society. If we have not given up this hope of progress as a caring society, are we willing to face our crisis and our lostness in the hope of moving, however precariously and painfully, towards a society in which more and more people know that they have worth – because they have a recognized place; because they have an opportunity of sharing in whatever livelihood is about? Are we ready to have another go at seeking to produce a society where *being a neighbour* is valued at least as highly as being a consumer. Or are we to conclude that the essence of liberty is the freedom to make money, if we can, regardless of what it does to our neighbours? And, if you take that view of liberty, does that imply that fraternity goes by the board except as ganging up among the successful to keep down the non-successful? If you move in that direction this has the effect of making fraternity among the unsuccessful into something that is likely to be regarded as conspiracy, criminality and riot. One man's fraternity is

74

another man's crime in that case. I think this is coming very close to threatening us. Also, equality becomes something you can never have – in any sense, and many people will never display. Because, if you grow up in an area of multiple deprivation you will show no signs of equality in education, capacity to take job opportunities even if they are there or of being able to contribute to any of the productive or expansive sides of society.

These, it seems to me, are the questions which the inner city forces upon us all. But the issues are very sharp, very bewildering and very disturbing. So it is not to be wondered at that most people cannot face them in all their complexity but only react very partially and instinctively. The outbreaks of violence in our inner cities from which we have suffered and which suggest there is more to come are very threatening indeed. I am very clear about this since I personally am scared stiff of ordinary confrontation, let alone violent confrontation! The problems which are increasingly revealed, and of which we are getting more and more analysis, look intractable. Who is able to unravel the tangled and interactive skeins? They range from the hard criminality surrounding drug-pushing to the sheer boredom or angry despair of a school-leaver who may be sharing his unemployment with four out of five of his peers, if he is white, and nine out of ten of his peers if he is black.

All this is bad enough in itself, so it is natural that many people want to see the inner cities as problems on their own, to be contained by increased policing, and to be assuaged by local ameliorative measures. But surely the inner cities are not a discrete and separate set of problems which we have among us and which some special bodies need to tackle. (You know, 'Let us have a brace of Lord Scarmans and that will sort it out.' Lord Scarman has done a very important job, but then everyone sort of sits back and thinks 'now the way ahead is clear'.) With increasing clarity the inner cities confront us not with the problems of the inner cities but with the problem that *we* are.

We are a society which is not sure where it is going, is not sure whether there is anywhere to aim at going, and is very unsure about whether you can aim at going anywhere or even try. For here again we come up against this disillusionment. To do things together, or to aim at things together, in the complexities of modern life, in industry and in trading conditions and so on, requires some strong form of state activity and some commitment to common planning as a desirable good (and not simply as a regrettable necessity). This sort of thing, as we all know, has for some time been widely discredited for a variety of reasons, which again one can only sketch quickly. Yet they must be indicated, for they have great force and have to be faced.

One reason for disillusionment about collective action and progress is ideological excesses. Too much has been claimed for what theories can do and for what collectivism can do and the problem of power has been ignored. Thus parties have captured power, especially in Eastern countries, and become tyrannies run by one tyrant. Then we have been disillusioned by what one might call various functional practicalities. There has been so much concentration on distribution and consumption that we have not concentrated enough on production. There has been an unrestrained and irresponsible demand for things like health services. Aneurin Bevin thought that if you set up a good service which served people at times of need you would mop up a pool of ill-health. But the way things have gone, we have actually multiplied ill-health, multiplied technological means of treatment and so on, and so we get the National Health Service appearing something like a bottomless pit of demand and cost. These problems have been accentuated by the shock of changes in trading conditions, which have moved out of our range of expectation any steady increase in affluence and cash resources. So if we are going to tackle problems together we have to face both the disciplines of limit *and* the cost of dealing with problems. We cannot simply buy ourselves out of problems with a little more money; we have to decide that some problems are more important to deal with than others and how we are to organize *together* and to face these problems and live with them.

I do not think that in our society we have worked out how to handle *negative* priorities in any other way than by a combination of two competitive approaches – the Market or sheer power. How does one *negotiate* negative priorities, for instance? We have no idea. All this has combined with a loss of will to face the problems of setting up something like a welfare state. We seem to have thought that if it was set up it would work in fifteen years and all would be well, whereas it is liable to take generations for something like that to work. You do not reconstruct society in the space of two or three parliamentary periods.

So, there are many reasons for uncertainty at least about collective actions. But it would seem to me that the urgent message of the inner cities to all of us is that, for the sake of our society as a whole and not just because of the dangerous problems of the inner cities themselves, we must try again. Try again, that is, at working out ways of common, collective and corporate action through the institutions of the state and of local government, which will shape our society and bring it together for finding a common future and a common sense of belonging, so that we may start to live with and live through the immense problems with which we are faced. Our problems, surely, are quite beyond the scope of the Market and the possibilities of privatization. All this takes a lot of arguing, but I mention just two things.

As some of you may know, I have been involved in arguments about the Transport Bill and the bus services and I have met Secretaries of State and other people and discussed with them as well as attending debates (even trying to make a speech myself). I still do not see how the people who want to privatize and deregulate the bus services think that multiple-deprived estates can be sources of the sort of profit that will persuade people to run bus services. It seems to me quite elementary. There is some belief in a sort of magic here – where do people on such estates get the cash that will actually help people to make profits so that they will run private bus services?

As for privatization in general – it does seem to me very odd that it should constantly be claimed that by selling shares in publicly owned enterprises where we can we are actually returning these industries to the people. It is certainly true that large public bureaucracies are not necessarily responsive to people. But the only people who can buy the shares are those who have the cash to buy them. Where are we going, then? *Not* in the direction of a general 'property-owning democracy'. Surely we are in fact heightening the divisions again?

Similarly it is not profits which need to go up – though we have to watch profitability – but progress which needs to be resumed. I suspect that as long as profitability, in a narrow and commercial sense, is made a near absolute criterion for nearly all important decisions, we shall not resume any sort of progress. Indeed we shall go deeper into the wilderness of confusion, alienation and violence. We are about to embark on a very serious discussion of the Fowler Green Paper on Social Services. The data about costs are formidable. But if we are not very careful we shall lose sight of the fact that the most likely effect of the review, at any rate as proposed, is simply to make worse-off people worse off. And what are the costs of that in our society?

Similarly, there is a great deal of evidence of what is called a cost-efficiency approach in both the Health Service and in education. No value seems to be given to the good will of the way hospitals as teams, or schools as teams, actually work. The whole thing seems to be very gravely dehumanizing. Perhaps we have been misled by the immense material progress of the Industrial Revolution in the West up until recently into the belief that progress means having more and more to consume. Perhaps we are now being reminded that real human progress – some of which has been achieved and the resumption of which is essential to the stability and value of our society – is growth in caring and in the attribution of worth to more and more of the members of society. The critical question really is – what dominates? Are we to be dominated and distorted by total emphasis on such matters as economic forces and the Market or are we to regain a sense of direction from a faith in men and women and their possibilities and requirements (which, of course, must accept the realities of economics and the Market but is not narrowly dominated by them)?

Now this is moving into a difficult area. Faith, as such, clearly cannot give us details, but surely it can, and must, give us direction. For instance, it seems to me that Christian faith underwrites and develops the conviction that men and women are meant to be free, that all human beings are of worth and are meant to share and to belong and to count; meant to have their own part to play in whatever relationships and livelihoods are available. Now that faith, that insight and that hope does not tell us directly about details and patterns of behaviour or about the workings of things like markets, banks or industries, distributive networks and all the rest of it. But surely our faith does and must warn us if we see any absolutizing of economic theories and explanations which lead people to declare, in answer to questions about effects and to cautions about pros-pects, that there is and can be no other way. Faith here surely joins up with prudence, prudence which has a wider vision than those who simply look at things from the point of view of the market. That joins up with common sense which surely refuses to be misled by mere theories and points out that there are more hard facts than those which are simply dealt with by Market theories and economic concerns. We should surely be the more ready to challenge the dominance of particular economic theories when the current ones show a steady bias in promoting the self-interest of those who promote them and a constant bias against statistically significant proportions of our people.

Another thing which seems to me to have to be questioned, partly on the basis of faith and partly on the basis of prudence and commonsense – which all come together – is what I might call a certain narrow selectiveness in the presentation of and appeal to facts. I suspect that this is to be seen – though I have no time to document this – in the present reiteration of claims that the economy is doing well. How can the economy be doing well when literally millions of our citizens are doing badly? The facts of deprivation, unemployment and alienation are surely quite as much hard facts as inflation rates, government borrowing and expenditure and defence – or are they? This, it seems to me, is where the question of faith and approach comes about – which once again returns us to the inner city.

Much of the current responses to the problems of the inner city seem to show a determination to reject or avoid those hard facts which challenge our very understanding of, and our visions of, our society. Thus, for example, black immigrants are seen as the principle cause of inner-city trouble. And from time to time people say 'Right! Send them home!' But home is here, possibly by a generation or two generations in some cases. In any case I think they are only focussing and magnifying our problems, the problems of the effect of multiple deprivation, of the effect of unemployment, of how to face living in a divided and pluralistic world – problems which we have anyway. How do we deal with our own divisions? So the problems cannot be sent home because they are 'at home' and they come home to us. We must face them together and not find diversionary scapegoats and illusionary simple solutions. The problems cannot go away and will not go away, therefore we have to live with them.

Or, again, there is a great deal of worry about how immigrants are changing what is called 'our way of life', will not fit into 'our way of life' and demand something in their own way. There are very difficult problems, for instance, about tension with regard to schools and education, in which neither side has a completely sound case. These face us with plurality, which has now become a feature of life and will remain so.

Or, on the religious front, people do get very worried about the growth in Mosques and gurudwaras: I have myself gone to work here in Manchester by a great and thriving mosque growing up while the church next door is falling down. But these problems are not to be sent home: they are very real problems in the sort of world we have now and it is no use, and not consistent with the hard facts, to make a slogan-like use of phrases like 'this should not happen, this is a Christian culture and a Christian country'. 'We must preserve our own culture.' As to this being a Christian country: quite plainly it is not. And unless the churches get adjusted to living in a missionary situation and work out how they can reproduce the vital Christian insights to contribute to a non-Christian country, we shall be no use.

As for the whole matter of culture – there are many people and villages in my part of the world whose culture is being totally undermined by what has happened to them economically. It may be inevitable, but there are as many problems within our own culture already in this country as those that have been introduced. What is the unified culture of an increasingly two-nations Britain?

So these problems will not go away. I think that rejection of our problems as they really impinge upon us and as they are presented to us through the inner city is shown most clearly by the claim that the way to deal with inner-city problems is chiefly by measures against criminality and against violence directly. That is to say: strengthen the police, create new offences and show determination. But consider the question of creating new offences. We are creating new offences in order to send people to prison, and possibly to prison for longer, when it is quite literally true that prisons are hopelessly full anyway. People will not look at these facts. I say *hopelessly* full, and I say it very firmly and urgently, because I have lately visited several prisons in my part of the world where the combination of prison officers and prisoners are coping in a manner which I can only call heroic with the most ridiculous and abominable conditions. Prisons are hopelessly full in the double sense that they are far too full yet people are proposing to find other offences for sending people to them; and, secondly, that most of this does no good whatever.

And nobody believes that it does any good. It would do still more harm if there was not some sort of common culture which manages to keep prisoners and prison officers together – though that does not mean that dreadful things do not happen out of sheer frustration. Yet we blithely go on thinking that the way to deal with our problems is to send more people to prison. That is one more example of the way in which the well-off simply refuse to face up to the problem of how we deal with the drop-outs. Do we lock them all up? I am afraid there is no room!

So, what are we going to do? If you turn the screw more tightly without dealing with the causes of pressures you simply heighten the pressures. The important point here, I think, is that you are putting quite impossible burdens on the police. I believe that the police are becoming increasingly a problem and a source of contention between parties because we will not face up to things and are unloading all our problems on to the police. It is perhaps not a mistake, or a chance, that the police have a blue uniform, because they seem to me to be the most amazing social litmus paper.

There is urgent need to tackle the divisions which are running through all our society here. People are getting polarized: either you are one hundred per cent for the police or you are in favour of riot and an enemy of public order and should resign. Or, all that can be said about the police is that they are the enemy. Now what of this, vis à vis the picture, which was not simply a romantic picture, of the police constable in the community? This, I know, remains or is being struggled back to in my own (if I may dare to call it so now) county, Durham. I have had some very moving conversations with miners and miners' wives about how they have lost all trust in the police because of what happened; though they are usually careful to say in Durham that it was those outsiders who caused the real trouble during the strike. (But then Durham is very good at putting things on to 'outsiders' – and so are a lot of other tribal areas, are they not?) Yet there is a real worry about the fact that we cannot trust the police any more, and a real worry on behalf of the police that they cannot be trusted any more. I think that we have to be very clear that we must not confuse our problems by landing them on the police. The police cannot and must not be asked to take all the burden of patrolling and controlling the wilderness of our social tensions and divisions. This is in any case a recipe for disaster, because the wilderness will get more violent and there will be need to show more and more strength, and then we shall go further and further in the direction of something which might be strangely and sadly like Fascism. Secondly, and more importantly, this is an intolerable burden on the police as persons. It points to something that the inner cities need to remind us all about: that everybody, however difficult it may seem at any given time, has to be considered as a person – especially when they are in groups.

What can you demand of persons, as well as what you can expect of them and what sometimes you do have to require of them? I think that all this shows up most sharply how the wilderness in our society has been further deepened by always expecting other people to deal with our problems.

Here we touch on something which is the source of some valid criticisms of the welfare state. In some aspects it does, undoubtedly, undermine ordinary caring and proper demand for responsibility. This has to be faced. On the other hand this criticism is far too rampant, and now serves as a refusal to face up to what the problems demand of us. It is no good paying more for the police in the belief that that will settle our problems and our share of responsibility. There are much wider issues to be faced for all of us.

So whether we happen to be inclined to the Left or inclined to the Right we are surely all condemned here, and all required to think again and act differently. I would suggest that the role of the police, and the issue around the police, perhaps makes it most clear how the inner city reflects and is part of our wilderness and how urgent it is that we face up to these deeper issues and do not just tinker, temporize, react and get more deeply entrenched in our narrow points of view which themselves get increasingly limited because we succumb more and more to the short-term pressures of self-interest and are trapped by fear and failure of vision.

Here I think we all have a battle to fight with the way in which at any rate most of the media behave; because the media encapsulate things in terms of polarizations which are already accepted. This means trapping us more and more in the problems we are creating for ourselves. How are we going to get the necessary new thinking, and new suffering, let alone new collaborating which is required to get us on and move us through this common wilderness?

So we come to the critical importance of the challenge to

faith and the challenge from faith. We are in a wilderness. We shall remain in a wilderness for at least the medium-term period. How do we understand, receive and react to our wilderness? Do we trap ourselves in increasing depression, fantasy and heightening conflict by a nostalgic longing to return – to return to some imagined prosperity and purpose of the past, to some effective operation of *laissez-faire* and competition, to some freedom where we (or at any rate enough of us) will be able to make sufficient money so that there will be enough to spill over and deal (presumably by charity) with all our problems. Are we trapped in this backward looking nostalgia, which is bound to be depressing and increasingly unrealistic?

Or can we begin to discover that the wilderness itself may be made hopeful by redeveloping common concerns, resuming direction and progress in the direction of what in religious language one calls a promised land? This, of course, is a promised land which never arrives in human affairs on this earth but is a constant compulsion to facing threats and problems as opportunities for improved caring, wider justice, increased freedom, and greater sharing in greater diversity. It is a promised land which provides a vision which ought to restore morale and collaboration, purposeful struggle and human celebration in the wilderness and in the midst of our problems and struggles.

I think that this is an immense challenge to the churches to work out and live by such a vision and a sense of direction. It is surely greatly to be hoped that the much heralded and publicized publication of the report of the Archbishop's Commission on Urban Priority areas will provide some sort of stimulus in this direction. It is to be hoped that it will not be pigeon-holed by church people saying: 'Well, here's a large document about inner-city areas, and those who are near to inner city areas have to deal with them but it is not a problem for the rest of us.'

In fact, it is going to pin-point a problem for us all. For surely there is no conflict in priorities or interest in our society today between the problems of our inner cities, the need to fight the blight in suburban areas and on many estates, the demands of rural poverty and the threat of the division of our society into two nations. All are part of one wilderness. Therefore they are parts of one common arena for the recovery of hope and direction in re-discovering and serving the common good. Clearly, for the churches, it is absolutely essential that we stay in the inner cities and reinforce our activities there for the sake of, and as part of, the response of the whole church to life in society and the nation as a whole. It is not a question of keeping up your missions in the inner city. It is a question of how to serve society in the struggles which confront us all. This should be hammered home very strongly. For the inner-city wilderness is an essential part of our calling and our service to society as a whole, to preaching the gospel as a whole, and to men and women throughout society.

What we have to find in and through the wilderness – by staying with it and facing it, (and I am sure it is there to be found if we are faithful, realistic and persevering) – is a renewal of a vision of being human together and of the chance of seeking greater, wider and deeper humanity. This, as I have argued at the beginning, involves the restoration of our sense of and our commitment to progress, progress which is not a growth in consumption but a growth in caring, not an extension of competition but an extension of community. The resumption of progress is not possible without a renewal of faith, of vision, of common commitment to seeking a truly common good. But it also has to be said that the resumption of such progress and the commitment to such progress – in however faltering a way – is actually extremely urgent; it is not a utopian irrelevance but a practical necessity. For, surely, anyone who is seeking to look into our future must feel at times very apocalyptic. Our present wanderings in the wilderness (as becomes increasingly evident) are liable to lead us, and to lead us fairly rapidly, from the wilderness to a desert, a desert of alienation, conflict and misery. We are already beginning to see signs of this. But we do not so far seem to have either the common insight or the common will to react with any common purpose or any common hope. Perhaps, as a first step, if we could help one another throughout society to see that the problems and the possibilities of the inner cities are our problems writ large – this might drive us together rather than increasingly separate us. But for this to happen, those of us who have faith (it may be faith drawn from a whole range of sources all the way from God to human faces – and of course anyone who believes in the incarnation will believe that God and human faces are more closely tied up than some people recognize), will have at all times to press these issues of a wider realism because we see a wider vision.

Surely we must challenge all the current over-simplifications and self-defeats by which efforts are directed to dealing with symptoms and recognition is refused to causes. It is easy to see why the deeper causes are not faced, for to face them demands repentence – real, drastic rethinking by all of us. But the more urgent the pressures can be shown to be, the better the chance of people being ready to rethink out of sheer necessity, always supposing that some realistic faith and some renewing vision is to be glimpsed which will encourage us in finding these new ways forward.

So, the challenge of the inner city to the churches, at any rate, seems to me to be clear. First of all our faith must sustain us in remaining in this wilderness and in reinforcing our resources in and commitment to this wilderness. Then, by facing with other people the threat that the wilderness will increasingly turn into a desert, we may struggle through to the regaining of hope. We may be turned from seeking false solutions worked out and imposed by others to working out realistic solutions discovered by and suffered through the common and corporate efforts and costs of ourselves and of all our neighbours together.

Faith, realistically alive, should enable us to develop our pilgrimages as human beings and to pick up our purpose as those who are called to give care and to receive care, called also to resume our progress as a society which has recaptured some common vision of being together and of pursuing things together. That seems to me to be the beginning of where the inner city pressures might lead us, if we have courage enough, faith enough and realism enough.

7

Faith in the City

'In keeping with his promise we are looking forward to a new heaven and a new earth, the home of righteousness.' This is what the author of the little New Testament book we call the Second Epistle of Peter wrote to his Christian hearers (II Peter 3. 13). What on earth did he mean? And whatever he meant, what ought it to mean for us that we are looking forward to a new heaven and a new earth, the home of rightousness? Would it be related to the prayer we use most frequently: 'Our Father, which art in heaven, hallowed be thy name, thy kingdom come, thy will be done, on earth as it is in heaven'? Certainly, if God's name *was* hallowed – that is, if God was fully treated, and responded to, as the God he is, the God of holiness, righteousness and steadfast love – if God's will *was* done – on earth as it is in heaven – then his kingdom would come and that would result in 'a new heaven and a new earth, the home of righteousness'. But what does our praying of this prayer mean for us now? What difference should our prayers make in what we do, what we aim for, what we should expect?

These are the questions which have more and more come up for me as we have continued to try to come to terms with *Faith in the City*, the report of the Archbishop's Commission on Urban Priority Areas, and as we have gone on asking ourselves what we should do about it and what differences it ought to make to us. I have been forced to the conclusion that the report *Faith in the City*, the contents of it, and the responses to it, especially those from the world outside the church, have put us on the spot with regard to the gospel.

I want to explore this with you with a great sense of urgency, excitement and hope. I hope therefore that you will patiently and carefully listen to me, as I shall have to take a bit of time to set out what I mean. But what I particularly want to do is to share with you my sense of urgency, excitement and hope. I have this sense because I know that when God puts us on the spot with regard to the gospel he does so because he is offering us newness, renewal and advance in the cause of his kingdom. This is a simple, clear and a basic matter of faith in God through our Lord, Jesus Christ.

The Bible makes it absolutely clear that God is a God of judgment. Of course he is a God of judgment, for he is the God of holiness, righteousness and steadfast love and he has a covenant or contract with his people to share in his being, his creation and his purposes. Therefore, out of his holiness, justice and love, he is bound to be against, to stand and act in judgment upon, everything that goes contrary to that holiness, justice and love. Creative and realistic love cannot confront sin without wrath. A passionate and powerful will and purpose of holy and just love must burn against everything that diminishes, distorts, perverts or interrupts the creative and loving possibilities of everything that exists and of every person that comes into being. So if there is a loving God related to this sort of a world he must be a God of judgment. And the Bible makes it abundantly clear that the living God is, indeed, a God of judgment.

But the good news, the gospel, is this. The one whom God has appointed to judge the world is precisely the one whom God has sent to be the sacrifice for the sins of the world. The

Judge of the world is the Saviour of the world. 'This is love, not that we love God, but that he loved us and sent his Son as an atoning sacrifice for our sins' (as we read in I John 4. 10). Or, as Paul puts it at the beginning of that tremendous eighth chapter of the letter to the Romans: 'Therefore, there is now no condemnation of those who are in Christ Jesus, because through Christ Jesus the law of the Spirit of life set me free from the law of sin and death. For what the law was powerless to do in that it was weakened by the sinful nature, God did by sending his own Son in the likeness of sinful man to be a sin offering. And so he condemned sin in sinful man, in order that the righteous requirements of the law might be fully met in us who do not live according to the sinful nature but according to the Spirit.'

It is not always easy to follow Paul, but the main thrust here, as elsewhere, is quite clear. What God was doing in Jesus Christ was at one and the same time to judge (condemn) sin 'in sinful man' and to set men and women free from sin to live according to the Spirit of God. Read the whole chapter and be very careful to note how, from v.18 onwards, Paul makes the amazing and glorious claim that this judging and saving activity of God in Jesus Christ through the Spirit has to do with the whole of creation. We are not dealing with some specialized divine transaction for the private salvation of some privileged individual souls. We are being presented with the pattern and dynamism whereby the God of all creation confronts what goes wrong in that creation, condemns all that is wrong, pays the price and makes the sacrifice for all that is wrong, and thereby sets us, and the whole of creation, free to enjoy and fulfil the purpose and riches of the love and the Spirit of God. God is righteous love and so must condemn, but God is sacrificial love and so can save. The purpose of divine condemnation is divine salvation.

This is the gospel, revealed in Jesus Christ, for the whole of creation. Hence, if and when we are put on the spot with regard to the gospel, we know that God is judging us and calling us in question in order to take us more deeply and more effectively into his saving purposes. This is why my faith in, and understanding of, God and his gospel in Jesus Christ gives me a sense of urgency, excitement and hope as I try to share with you some hard and testing things with which *Faith in the City* is confronting us.

It is like this. We – that is the Church of England in particular – really have to show we are serious now. For the report *Faith in the City* has, in a particularly sharp and focussing way, *shown up the scale of the problem*. This scale of the problem is both the scale of the problem in and for society and the scale of the problem in and for the church. We, each and every one as individuals, naturally and necessarily live in our own small world. We have to get on with whatever it is we have to get on with, whether it is people to enjoy or people to endure, jobs to do or jobs to look for, money to raise, money to spend or money to do without – and so on. But you and I are Christians, committed Christians, active members of a living section of the church of Christ. So we have been called to have conscious and active dealings with the living God of the whole world and to be both hearers and sharers of that God's good news, the gospel which is spoken to all in judgment so that all may be saved. Just sometimes, therefore, in our own small worlds, God may speak to us sharply but lovingly about our world as a whole and about our calling under him, which is entirely dependent upon his grace and power for service in and witness to that world. Just now I believe that God is using the report *Faith in the City* to say to us two things. The first is: 'Look, the society and nation of which your own small world is a part is in danger of becoming one hell of a mess and you must face up to it.' The second is: 'Look, the church to which you belong is much smaller and more insignificant than you think and in danger of becoming increasingly inefficient and irrelevant in its service of the kingdom and you must face up to it.' Of course, as I have already explained, God is saying these words of judgment and questioning not to condemn us but to set us free for deeper faith, deeper service and deeper joy. But he is speaking very sharply to us, which is why I have such a sense of urgency. At the same time it is the God and Father of Our Lord Jesus Christ who is speaking so sharply to us, the God who is judge in order to be saviour. Which is why I am absolutely sure we may and must respond to the urgency and sharpness with excitement and hope. God is getting at us because he intends to do new things with us and new things for us. He is putting us on the spot with regard to the gospel.

Which is where I return to the *scale* of the problems brought into focus for us in the church by *Faith in the City*. The report makes it quite clear that there are large concentrations of people in our country who are doing badly in terms of ordinary survival and flourishing; they have very poor chances of doing better for themselves, and the way things are going in society at large causes them steadily to do even worse. If you are poor, you are being made poorer – and this is the case for tens of thousands of men, women and children concentrated thickly in the seven great conurbations of our country ('Tyne and Wear is the one in our part of the world), some of them in the inner city and some of them in the suburban and fringe housing estates which cluster around them. The poor and deprived in our Urban Priority Areas are, so to speak, concentrated examples of what our society is doing to those who are not in the mainstream of the way in which society as a whole at present flourishes and makes and uses its wealth.

The scale of the problem does not only lie in its sheer statistical size (that is the number of people actually involved) nor in its concentration in particular geographical areas (so that the problems are self-reinforcing). It lies also in the size of the comparative gap between the poorness of the poor and the richness of the rich or the well-doing of the well-to-do. This, of course, is of immense psychological, social and human importance in a society where everything, not least the media, is concentrated on promoting and extolling and developing consumption. Where are you in an enterprise culture expressed in a consumer society if you have a negative chance of being enterprising and no spare resources for consumption? You are failing as well as suffering. And that dimension of the scale of the problem is shown in the health statistics. Look at pages twelve and thirteen in the main report and you will see that a person's chances of dying tomorrow are very much higher if he or she lives in Gateshead or Sunderland than if he or she lives in Harrogate or Highgate. Life simply gives up much earlier. Everything about one's experiences of life, one's expectations of life and one's chances of and in life are clearly and demonstrably shaped by that coming together of circumstances which produce and maintain the Urban Priority Areas and the deprived housing estates. And, as the Report points out, these dehumanizing conditions are maintained or accelerated *by human decisions*.

Consider the two following very important statements from chapter 1 of the Report.

In the nation as a whole since the end of the post-war period the rich have got richer and the poor poorer. Similarly, the Oxford Studies of Occupational Mobility show that chances of mobility for men of working-class origin polarized between 1972 and 1983 as the opportunities for upward mobility continued, while the chances of unemployment also rose. Again Chris Hamnett's study of change in housing tenure concludes that, as between owner-occupation and local authority renting, there has been 'an increasing degree of social polarization'. The analysis by David Eversley and

94

Ian Begg demonstrates that polarization also divides the Urban Priority Areas from the rest of Britain. It involves a triple process of decision; by individuals competing for advantages in jobs, housing, schools and services; by governments offering mortgage relief and withholding investment from blighted districts; and by enterprises rationally investing where consumer power is greatest and growing.

A little later the Report goes on:

Meanwhile at this point we would emphasize above all that the inner city and the peripheral estate are creatures of the whole of society, not simply of their inhabitants. Urban Priority Areas are explained effectively only by recognition that they have emerged out of human decisions, whether through political authority, business management or individual choice. While appreciating the external forces of world-wide recession, currency movements and international markets, we must also insist that there is a collective responsibility for the problems of poverty and inequality that we have described (pp. 23ff.).

So, 'there is a collective responsibility for the problems of poverty and inequality' with the dimensions and on the scale described. Well, is there? This is where we, as Christians, are put on the spot with regard to the gospel. How does the gospel help and direct us in loving our neighbours in this sort of a world? How does our understanding and living of the gospel help us to preach the gospel, in this sort of a world? What would the gospel have us do in warning and helping society for its own health and future when it is producing and maintaining this sort of a world in its inner cities and elsewhere?

You will remember the dialogue which occurred after Jesus had told the parable of the Good Samaritan. Jesus said, 'Which of these three do you think was a neighbour to the man who fell into the hands of robbers?' The expert in the law replied, 'The one who had mercy on him.' Jesus told him, 'Go and do likewise' (Luke 10. 36ff.). How do we 'have mercy' on neighbours who are not just individuals who have fallen into a ditch after having been attacked by robbers but thousands of people who are in 'the ditch' they are in because of the structures of society, because of the way things are going in society and because of a multiplicity of decisions of all sorts of 'gangs' at all sorts of levels? If the gospel is the good news of the power and presence of God for judgment and salvation and it is for all, then surely we cannot ignore this plight of theirs whch comes very close to determining what they make of life and what life makes of them. Nor can we ignore the reasons for which they are in it.

Admitedly, this does put us on a very awkward spot because we clearly have very few clues as yet about how we should reply or respond to pressures like these. But the awkward spot might turn out to be a highly promising and exciting spot if we can stay on it and face its challenges together. For there is potentially a very close connection between finding realistic and effective ways of bringing signs of love to neighbours who are trapped in thousands, and trapped far more by social structures than individual sins, and regaining our power to preach the gospel with effectiveness and and to society as we have it today. It is all a matter of *messages*.

The gospel is the message that God is and he is as he is in Jesus. There is therefore the offer of being saved from the sin which distorts and destroys and of being saved for that sharing in the love of God and of one another which enables growth and promises fulfilment. But this is not a message which many people can hear or which we are very good at sharing. People, many of them, say in a vague sort of way that somehow or other they believe in some sort of God but they do not find church talk or biblical talk, nor the behaviour of Christians and religious activities, in any way credible, relevant or engaging. The messages which people in Urban Priority Areas or peripheral housing estates receive and which dominate their lives and their approach to, and expectations of, life are clear enough. They are that you do not count, you are a problem, society does not want you, school cannot prepare you for a job, official help is liable to be given, even when available, grudgingly and with suspicion. The well-heeled ignore the ill-helped and go on their way. Society is for those who can do well out of society and thus do well in society. The rest, if they are not treated as drop-outs, are certainly treated as left-outs.

There is, therefore, literally no reason on earth why people who suffer from the major problems of our society, or people who are deeply concerned about these problems, should pick up messages of good news about a God who confronts all with the judgment of love so that all might be freed for the salvation and sharing of love. Everything is programmed to give quite different messages – and the churches who claim to be seeking to convey this gospel message do not seem to be plugged into the programming side of society at all or engaging with the messages by which society lives. Instead they run their own small shows in their own narrow ways.

This is where we come to the other hard thing which I believe God is saying to us in order to release us and renew us for new freedoms and advances in the service of the gospel and of the kingdom. *Faith in the City* throws sharply into relief just how thin on the ground we are and just how we are often pretty irrelevant to everyone save ourselves. Start with figures, which do not mean everything, but which mean something. Paragraph 2.25 states that 'For the Church of England nationally, the average adult church attendance in each "parish" on a Sunday is 119, representing 1.4% of an average parish population of 8,410. In Urban Priority Area parishes the equivalent figures are an average of 90 adults attending out of a parish population of 10,560 (0.85%). We may compare this with a table in the *Tyne and Wear Christian Directory* published in 1986 by MARC Europe, a painstaking assembly of information about all Christian churches and organizations in the five local government districts which used to make up the county of Tyne and Wear and three of which (Gateshead, South Tyneside and Sunderland) fall in our diocese. Table 3 is an area summary of church membership and indicates that 11% of the total population are churchgoers and just over a quarter of these are Anglican. This gives a Church of England church membership of 3% of the total population. Elsewhere it is calculated that average attendance at church on any one Sunday is about 50% of church membership. So this would give a figure of 1.5% of the population in church on a Sunday, compared with the *Faith in the City* estimate of 1.4% for the overall parishes and 0.85% in an Urban Priority Area. This suggests that there is some rough accuracy about both calcuations, although, as we all know, numbers are very tricky things.

I think we can be properly reminded that our active worshippers and church members are about three in a hundred of our population and neighbours. We also need to be reminded that although we call ourselves the Church of England, we are actively about one quarter of those worshipping and congregating as Christians in the area. I know, of course, that there are other considerations about how people more broadly feel, and sometimes act, about belonging to, or being related to, the Church of England. However, I think it very important that we are as clear and as realistic as possible about the strength of what might be called our basic and reliable troops. This sort of realism would seem all the more important in the light of certain matters of finance.

We shall shortly be accepting, I hope with real satisfaction and thankfulness, the one hundreth annual report of the diocese of Durham. On the financial side we shall be registering the most encouraging fact that the parishes have raised the sums asked of them to an extent never before achieved. In fact, on the total size of the sum required, the shortfall is really negligible – and money is still coming in. I think we can truly say that we have never done better. At the moment there is financial soundness and no crisis. Just the moment, therefore, to listen to the *krisis* or judgment of God! You will note from the second paragraph of my introduction to the annual report that the sum we so triumphantly raised represents *just under one half* of what it costs to keep our present religious paraphernalia on the ground, including, most especially, the stipends and housing of our priests and other ministers.

Thus if we take a realistic view of ourselves, the Church of England in the diocese of Durham as it actually is on the ground, we are bound to say that we are a struggling and thinly spread small minority (about 3 in 100) who are a minority even of those who practise the Christian religion in relation to church-going and congregation-belonging, and who barely half pay for the maintenance of the religious plant and personnel that we at present have. *This* is the body which is put on the spot with regard to the gospel by the facts and challenges of *Faith in the City*.

Moreover the challenge is further heightened by the secular responses to *Faith in the City*. Now, many political and social action groups and charities and other organizations have said: 'Here we can and must take the Church of England seriously. Now it is paying attention to what is really going on, how people really struggle and suffer and the problems that urgently need facing in society. Now we can see that perhaps they do have a realistic bit of good news and a realistic commitment to it in relation to the actual society we really do live in.' So we, the Church of England, are expected to deliver – what? I think

I may say without blasphemy and as a genuine prayer, 'My God, we *are* in a spot'.

Which is where we come back to my matter of simple faith that I set before you at the beginning of this speech and search. God has put us on this spot. I am convinced that if God is knocking us as hard as he seems to be, then he really has something urgent and exciting to say to us and share with us. What it is we shall have to discern together and to receive together. But I believe that it is something to do with re-discovering the power and the direction of the kingdom. Further, as part of doing this we shall need both to repent of, and to fight against, idolatry.

The power of the kingdom is that severe love of God which fights against all that distorts and diminishes the godly and loving possibilities of men and women and of the world. It is therefore judgment against all that men and women do, or allow to remain, that distorts and diminishes one another and the world. At the same time, the kingdom of God is the power of healing and saving love which condemns in order to enable fresh starts, calls in question in order to renew and suffers evil and frustration in order to build up community and goodness. The direction of the kingdom is, therefore, indeed towards 'a new heaven and a new earth, the home of righteousness'. This direction we are called to pursue in the face of the facts pre-sented to us in *Faith in the City*. To this end we must be ready to have both the priorities and the practices of our church life altered. That is the way of renewal.

As we prepare for this, we are surely challenged to fight idolatry. First of all we have to be set free from making idols of our church structures, our church buildings, church practices and our particular church identities. Nothing in the church properly exists for us. All exists for God, for his kingdom and for the world. It is because it so exists that it exists as a means of grace for us. We have therefore to find ways to be concerned less with our survival and preservation and more with the direction of God's kingdom, the preaching of the gospel to our neighbours in ways which they can begin to hear and the pressing of God's judgment upon society so that it may be given healing and hope.

For we need urgently to escape from our own religious idolatry so that we can be set free to fight for the kingdom against the idols of our society, those idols which are threatening to destroy our society by divisiveness and our world by pollution and exhaustion. They are the age-old idols of riches and self and power for one's own – old idols erected into unbridled pursuit of consumption, unrestrained competition and unfeeling individualism by specious dogmas about the way the world must be run, regardless of the costs to both community and the future.

So it is under pressures and with opportunities something like these that we have to approach all our agendas in the diocese. *Faith in the City* is important in itself – but it is even more important because it focusses our minds about what the church is really for, what it is at the moment really like, and the sort of world we really have to operate in. God is putting us on the spot about the gospel. We must be ready therefore for a good deal of discomfort and challenge, given to help us on to excitement and hope. And it *is* urgent.

The gospel needs to be preached, it needs to be preached *now* and it needs to be preached in such ways that people have some chance of picking up the message. On the one hand thousands of people are getting nothing but messages of worthlessness and hopelessness. This is blasphemous and contrary to the love and good news of God. On the other hand so much in our society and in our own behaviour is simply idolatrous and destructively self-centred. We must receive the grace of God to free ourselves from idols and to witness against the idols of society.

In particular we are called, I am sure, to see just how frail, over-stretched and thin on the ground our church really is. This is *not* to condemn us to fear and desperation. It is the purpose and pressure of God to prevent us from attempting the impossible so that we may be freed to do the worthwhile. Do we need this building any more, ought we to keep all these separate parishes going, why do we burden the good men and women we have with impossible tasks of pastoralia and main-tenance, when will we really be ready to work practically with other Christians – and so on?

Both this speech of mine and the presentation you will shortly receive are simply first stabs at an agenda which God is offering us, an agenda which can set us free from being struggling survivals of an obsolescent Church of England into being both a close-knit and a far-flung network of servants and heralds of the always forward-looking, always hopeful and always caring kingdom of God.

PART THREE

God and the Future

8

The God of Freedom and the Freedom of God

Freedom is an urgent practical issue in our society and in our politics. On the one hand, freedom of the individual is seen as gravely threatened by the interference of the state in too many spheres and by the collective organization characteristic of socialism. It is also claimed that unless the individual is set free for activities maximizing profits in a free market there is no way out of our current economic depression and malaise. On the other hand, it is urged that talk of freedom is a bad joke at the expense of the increasing number of unemployed and others (such as the aged) who cannot help themselves and who are slipping into increasing poverty and deprivation. It is also claimed that the freedom of the individual is under growing threat from the increasingly centralized forces of law and order which are marshalled in the face of mounting social turbulence. Further, the very idea of the 'Free Market' is said to be highly questionable in the face of the activities of monopolies, cartels and multi-national corporations, let alone in relation to those who, because of their poverty, have scarcely any individual purchasing power. There seems to be some *prima facie* force in most of the arguments marshalled on both sides. Also, there seem to be as many reasons for questioning the efficiency and freedom of socialist societies as there are for

105

questioning the justice and long-term stability of capitalist ones. This suggests that a reasonable subject for a Hibbert Lecture is to examine the idea of freedom in relation to biblical and Christian ideas of God. If one believes in the God who is witnessed to in the Bible and worshipped in the Christian tradition, what light is thrown on our perplexitites about, and prospects of, freedom?

A remarkable feature of the God of the Bible is his expectation of responsibility and response. He may be (and increasingly so as he is perceived to be the God of the whole universe) mysterious, inscrutable and holy, to be approached and revered in fear and awe, but the humanity and the responsibility of his worshippers are in no way diminished by their relationship with him. In the stories of Abraham and of Moses the basic note is struck which eventually resonates in the saying, for example, of Micah: 'God has told you what is good, and what is it that the Lord asks of you? Only to act justly, to love loyalty, to walk wisely before your God' (6.8). Cultic practices and the observance of ritual rites are all part of such a free and personal response of obedience, loyalty and justice to God in his holiness and his covenant relationship. Where this response is lacking and the rules and rituals have become the expression of a religion socially observed, but not reaching out into either the living reality of God or the living practices of society at large, then they are denounced in the name of God both by the prophets and by Jesus.

It is on this basis that the great prophets Isaiah, Jeremiah and Ezekiel are able to face, explain and find hope through the catastrophes which overcome Israel and Judah. These disasters are seen as punishment for turning away fom God which was manifested not only in the worship of false gods, but also in the blatant practice by both king and courtiers of exploitation and injustice. Seen in this way it was possible to regard the catastrophes not as the last word on the people of Israel, but as

106

episodes of disaster and disobedience from which they could be eventually saved and restored when they repented and responded to God's presence and grace. Thus the prophets could look forward to a king who would rule justly and the messianic hope was born. An example of this is: 'Then a root shall grow from the stock of Jesse ... he shall judge the poor with justice and defend the humble in the land with equity; his mouth shall be a rod to strike down the ruthless, and with a word he shall slay the wicked' (Isaiah 11.1ff.). These verses and many others like them contribute to a vision of a society of freedom, justice and peace. This vision and hope arises from faith in a God who has purposes of justice and peace which he is pursuing through men and women who have the opportunity of responding to him in freedom and obedience. Despite failures the hope and the vision remain realistic and compelling because God is persistent in pursuing his purposes in the face of disobedience and disaster.

He is thus a God of freedom in the sense that he requires a response of his chosen and covenanted people and that this assumes (or creates) their ability and responsibility to make a choice in response to their calling and to make their contribution to the keeping of the covenant. He is also a God of freedom in the sense that his purpose in pursuing his covenant with, and commitment to, Israel is seen more and more in terms of establishing an ideal community or kingdom of peace and justice and so of freedom and enjoyment. He is further a God of freedom in the third sense that he has the power and the will (understood increasingly as the power and will of love) not to be turned aside from his free purposes for the freedom of his chosen people by their failures in response and consequent loss of freedom. What he has done in freeing his people from slavery in Egypt he will continue to do in pursuit of his free purpose for their freedom in his kingdom and community.

For the Christian, Jesus is the endorsement, the reinforcement and the redirection of this faith and hope in God, experienced and explored in the service of a community and kingdom of justice and peace, freedom and love. Jesus had proclaimed that the kingdom of God was at hand, he had worked signs and wonders, taught the parables of the kingdom and disturbed his contemporaries with the claims and the powers of that kingdom. When the kingdom of this world (the civic authorities of Rome and the religious authorities of Judaism) had combined to get rid of him, they had not succeeded. Crucified and buried, he was then known to be risen and alive for ever and believed in as 'at the right hand of God'. That is to say that he is known to faith as the very expression, evidence and power of God's kingdom, as God's way of being with us and God's way of working for us. This faith was rapidly universalized. God's community and kingdom was seen as being open 'to all nations'. Thus, although in its various forms Christianity has never succeeded in fully living up to faith in God through Jesus Christ in actual practice, the thrust of this faith has always been that God is at work through the whole earth and the whole of history to enable and evoke the response and responsibility of freed men and women. The divine calling is to contribute to and thus to enjoy God's kingdom and community of justice, peace and love. It is this pattern and purpose and power of God which is held to be persistently at work in history, through history and beyond history.

Much in human history seems to deny this or work against this, not least in the history and behaviour of religious persons and institutions, including, with regrettable obviousness, much of the history and behaviour of the Christian church and churches. But Christians, reinforced in their faith in God through Jesus Christ, his resurrection and the sending of the Spirit, share the prophetic discernment that God remains persistently and patiently at work, not least through the very disasters and disappointments of history, to press on with his work of evoking from men and women a free response to his being, a share in his purpose of love and freedom, and a ready collaboration in the building of his community. Thus there is involved in Christian faith a claim about reality, inherited from the prophets and as vindicated in Jesus. This is the claim that history can, must and will be related to the kingdom and community of God. But this is not an invitation to, or a licence for, any form of historicism. That is to say it does not admit or encourage the belief that history has one clear pattern or direction which is discernible, achievable or inevitable. To clamp a pattern on history or to claim that we have the esoteric knowledge which gives us the vital clue to history is to misunderstand both the God of freedom and the freedom of God and so to misunderstand the human predicament and the human contradiction. Our lives in history are not the substance of the kingdom of God, only the material for it.

What is involved here is a profound question about our understanding of God. God is not the mastermind of a vast construction activity, planned in computerized fashion from the beginning and moving on inevitably to a predetermined and preconceived end. He (and She and It – for how can gender pronouns be sufficient for the mystery of God?) is much more like a master artist (and a mistress artist). This mysterious artist is committed in passion, righteousness and holiness to an infinite creative activity, launched by love and seeking, making and feeling ways forward by freedom and in freedom. The movement and the struggle is through tremendous risks, to the fulfilment of a commitment, a vision and a hope which will establish a community and a kingdom commensurate with the initial love, the consequent cost and the subsequent promise. Nothing is certain, but everything is possible. Such committed and constructive openness is the basic condition of freedom and love.

Faith of this sort in a God of this sort has an immediate bearing on the urgent practical issues of our society and our politics. For it calls for a recovery of nerve about the possibilities of politics and the possibilities of progress in our society. This is because such a faith sets us free from the determinism and despair of dialectics and from the apathy of randomness and powerlessness. If our lives in the world are open to God then we need not be trapped in dialectic or lost in randomness. Yet these are the only alternatives which seem to be perceived in this country at the moment. We are caught in a politics of confrontation which is shaped (whether consciously or unconsciously) by a slogan or two from vulgar Marxism. Everything is to be understood and dealt with in terms of conflict and power struggle between the class of capitalist individualists on the one hand and the class of collectivized wage earners on the other. This view is taken as much by the Right as by the Left.

The attempt to construct a welfare state which was entered into so enthusiastically after the 1939–45 war has run into acute difficulties and many disappointments. These difficulties and disappointments are diagnosed by the Right as being the inevitable consequences of attempts at socialism. The malaise of the welfare state and the inability of this country to break out of recession are seen to be symptoms of the same disease as holds Eastern Europe in its condition of tyranny and inefficiency. This is the disease of socialism and collectivization which inevitably destroys economic efficiency, innovation and advance. Before this became evident and in the euphoria and relief of the immediate post-war period socialism was seen as the way forward. Indeed, at the height of the socialist enthusiasm and fervour it was held that 'There is Only One Way Left'. This way has proved a dead end. It has led to neither freedom nor economic expansion, nor social and industrial flexibility. The evident failure of 'Only One Way Left' has now made it clear, so it is firmly believed and preached, that 'There Is Only One Way Right'. So there is no realistic alternative to the new conservatism, and anyone who suggests there is, is a romantic, an incompetent sentimentalist and a wet. But this is simply vulgar Marxism in reverse. The Marxist doctrine speaks of the spurious freedom of the bourgeoisie being at the expense of the real freedom of the workers, which freedom is alone universalizable in the eventual classless society after the withering away of the state. The new Right have a diagnosis and faith which is the mirror image of this. The spurious freedom which is to be resisted is that of the socialist collective of the workers which has been attempted at the expense of the true freedom of the bourgeois individualists. It is *this* freedom which is alone universalizable after the market has been liberated to work its wonders, and there emerges the freedom of a property-owning democracy, while the state has been reduced to the absolute minimum.

These two myopic and mirror-image views of the world now dominate such political thinking as there is and apparently mesmerize all those (almost certainly the majority) who do not find either view convincing or hopeful, not least because they are really one view and feed on one another in sustaining their respective claims to be 'realistic'. If you view the dialectic from the Right then the miners are to be utterly defeated, for they represent the shock troops of militant socialist workers, as is evidenced by their being led by a militant revolutionary. Any attempt to suggest that there are human and communal factors independent of this and mixed up in this is dismissed as an utter failure to face up to the realities of power and the urgent need to prevent revolution. If you view the dialectic from the Left then the miners are the heroes of the revolution and the police are the shock troops of bourgeois repression. Any

111

attempt to suggest that there are, independently of this and mixed up in this, urgent and difficult questions about obsolescence, economic recession and wealth production, flexibility and the communal and personal stresses of change is dismissed as an utter failure to face up to the realities of power and the urgent need to promote revolution.

That we are, at any rate for the moment, trapped in this dialectic understanding is evidenced by the current embarrassment and ineffectiveness of the 'soft' Left and the 'wet' Right. Social Democrats, whether in the Labour Party or outside it, often seem to behave as if they had at least a sneaking feeling that the hard Left are the only real and realistic activists. At least they cannot be challenged head on. Similarly, Conservatives with a sense of the strong Conservative traditions for corporate caring and an organic approach to many social problems seem hardly to have the courage of their convictions and a sneaking feeling that the market monetarists are the only realists. This means that more and more people who feel that the dialectic, whether viewed from the Right or from the Left, offers much more confrontation and misery than real promise or hope, are driven towards the view that politics are hopeless so that one must either take refuge in apathy or else invest ones energies in some single issue which is then identified as the central issue of political and human significance. There is also a steady growth in violence, because of frustration over helplessness, of fury over lack of progress on *the* central vital issue or because of the breakdown of social bonds and social discipline, since society and community as locally experienced are simply not felt to be holding together or working together for anything worthwhile or hopeful.

All this shows how urgent it is that we in this country should develop a liberation theology of our own. This would be a theology which struggled, worked and experimented to develop an understanding of the God of freedom and the freedom of God which effectively related the biblical tradition of this God to the actual state of affairs in this country and thus helped both in renewing faith in God and also in renewing our politics. We need to rediscover that we were not mistaken when we committed ourselves, with a considerable degree of consensus, to working out a welfare state which would substantially contribute to setting people free from unnecessary ill-health, hopeless poverty or acute want and which would make some movement, however slight, along the path to more justice, more caring and less thoughtless and ignored exploitation. We have been checked and we have made many mistakes, so there is much to learn and much to invent. We have also to work out our understanding and practice for the next stage of our political and social search with an awareness that progress towards justice and social peace requires much sharper choices than we might like and is under much more difficult conditions of wealth creation than we are accustomed to reckon with.

What essays in various aspects and forms of liberation theology would do is to remind those of us who are Christians that God has an investment in the human project and that we are called to collaborate with him in furthering this project. By responding to such reminders and by working out what they practically require we would be witnesses of the possibility and the concern of God to those who reject or ignore him as a possible or hopeful reality. We would also be making our contribution to a renewed common search for progress in the pursuit and building of a common good.

British essays in liberation theology would not be mere echoes or reflections of liberation theology elsewhere. As I learnt from my contacts with some of those who developed liberation theology in Latin America and South-East Asia, it would not be in the spirit of liberation theology if they were. As an article published in the Philippines in Manila in 1971 puts it: 'The question is not 'How can we adapt theology to our needs?' rather, 'How can our needs create a theology which is our own?' Liberation theology rises out of the particular needs of a particular country for hope in relation to justice, peace and love. It is an attempt to put into practice the biblical and prophetic insight that God is to be found in what puts pressure on *our* humanity wherever we are and that God is active and available to move *us* forward, whoever we are, in the direction of justice, peace and love and so to catch us up in our particularities into the work of his kingdom. This is to be encountered and responded to in this world, so that we may be part of the eventual fulfilment which lies in God's future, God's heaven and God's community.

Thus, while British liberation theology will take some of the diagnoses of Marxism very seriously, it will not in any way be dominated by Marxism. We must work out our own liberation theology, related to our needs and to what we can discern through seeking to be faithful to the God of the prophets and the God and Father of our Lord Jesus Christ. The main thrust of this liberation theology will, I am clear, include the following.

We must resume our search for progress in the direction of justice, increase of democratic participation and the organization of systematic and social caring. To give up the central concerns of the welfare state and the Beveridge Report because we have run into difficulties is sheer faithlessness and inhumanity. To return to the ethics of nineteenth-century entrepreneurial individualism is either nostaligic nonsense or else a firm declaration that individual selfishness and organized greed are the only effective motivations for human behaviour, or a mixture of both. In the name of the God of the Bible and of Jesus Christ we must challenge this and confront it. We must admit that the way forward is neither obvious nor easy but in the name of God and for the sake of our humanity we must insist that we cannot go backward into a twenty-first century version of the nineteenth century. That way destruction and misery lie.

Secondly, we must insist on the urgent reality and relevance of the judgment of God. To ignore the poor or to claim that they cannot be counted into society until we have made more money or that we must lay greater burdens on them to ensure that they are more ready to work at any cost is morally questionable, prudentially dangerous (for how much pressure will how many take for how long?) and a deliberate declaration of no sympathy or compassion with their plight. A society which does such things deliberately and refuses to recognize that that is what it is doing is a society which is tearing itself apart and heading for turbulence and disaster. Such a society can be no base for the learning and experimenting we have to undergo together to find a viable way forward into an uncertain and pretty tough future.

Thirdly, a liberation theology will search for ways of innovation, experiment and risk. For example, trade unions will have to risk new forms of wages, flexibility and new forms of work sharing. Management will have to risk new forms of participation and of limitation of privileges and salaries for themselves and their directors. Many unthinkable things (e.g. maximum and minimum wages) will have to become thinkable, including, probably, government risks over decentralization and regionalization.

Fourthly, liberation theology will have to work at building up communities of endurance around a celebration of the gospel of God who is committed to our world, our society and our future for the sake of his kingdom. For it is certain that we shall have much to endure, including uncertainty, turbulence, violence and people feeling that there is no hope and no way forward. In God and under God this is not true, but sometimes the only way of fighting through to a way forward will be communities of endurance who can hope against hope, as the

115

prophets did. Yet hope which is realistically and resolutely based on the living God who is the God of freedom can, through judgment, innovation and endurance, lead us again and again into further progress into the freedom of God which is the liberation of ourselves and our society in the direction of justice, peace and love.

9

Prospects for Peace

I am finding myself more and more forced to face and take a stand on questions and problems about which I am uncertain what to say or what to believe. The problem then is what to say and believe and do when you are uncertain what to say, believe and do. It is not possible to fall back on silence. For the problems are there and very urgent. Nor is it possible to speak with simple certainty about answers, for neither certainty nor clear answers are yet available. Yet it *is* certain that the problems and questions are there and that they are pressing and, often, threatening. We are threatened by the Bomb, by the miseries of prolonged unemployment, by growing violence and so on. What then to do? For me, it is an axiom of faith that *God is in reality*. That is to believe and say two things. First it is to believe that God really is and really is God. That is to say that there is this power behind things, presence within things and promise beyond things who is concerned for justice, truth and love. It is also, along with the faith of the Bible, to believe that God is to be met with, learnt about and served through the realities with which we are confronted in our daily lives and in the life of the world at large. Therefore faith in God obliges me to face questions and problems which are real, urgent and threatening. This is so not because this faith provides me with answers to such problems but because this faith commands me to seek and serve God in and through these urgent problems which put question marks over the lives and futures of all of us.

All this applies as I look at the questions: What are our chances of not being destroyed? Can we avoid the unintended extermination of the human race? This is a reality if ever there was one and therefore a problem through which, for the believer, God must be saying something to us and in which God must offer some resources and sense of direction. In any case, it is a clear enough common human concern whatever we believe and however we believe whatever it is that we do believe.

I have been reinforced in my determination to sort out some ideas and suggestions in the face of this great problem by two personal experiences. The first is that I was recently visited by the black editor of a paper in South Africa. Naturally we discussed all those issues of South Africa which are so constantly before us on our television screens. But in the course of conversation he made it quite clear to me that deeply troubling as the problems of South Africa are for him and his people and for all the people in that part of the world, what he called 'the bottom line' of the human problem and, for him, the bottom line in the issue of any sort of faith in any sort of God, is what is to be said, believed and hoped about nuclear war and the prospects of our avoiding it. One could have no better example of the way in which the issue of nuclear weapons dwarfs, or at any rate, puts in a particular perspective, all our other urgent human problems. My second set of personal experiences is to do with my six grandchildren now aged from four years old downwards. My joy and pleasure and pride in them have forced my thoughts sharply to questions about the future. What future do my grandchildren really have? But it is very important to note that what I have to say is a personal attempt to state where at the moment one struggling Christian stands.

It is not any sort of representative statement on behalf of 'the church'. Indeed, one thing that has to be taken into account in attempting any personal statement is that neither 'the church' nor the various churches have any simple, clear and agreed approach to the issues involved in the nuclear arms race and the preservation of peace or at least the avoidance of war. Hence all I can do is to make a personal contribution on the basis of struggling faith, a groping discernment and an imperfect obedience. Thus we come to the question, 'What are the prospects for peace?'

The first answer – and it is one which must be carefully understood and interpreted – is that there are no prospects for peace. First, a simple glance at history shows us that conflict is endemic between people, groups, tribes, nations and empires. Secondly, there is no agreement about the contents of positive peace. Peace is a dream, a hope and an aim but we have no clear idea of what it would look like or feel like. Further, there are no prospects of providing one overall understanding of peace by the rapid emergence of a shared powerful vision or by the enforcing of some one notion of peace by conquest or conversion. When one comes to think of it, this is no bad thing. Given our experience of the practice of totalitarianism both in religious attempts to enforce one vision and understanding and in the actual results of a political ideology which believes it has a full and sole vision of what human living together ought to be, we can see how important an openness and variety on this issue of positive peace is. Further, if I may add one more comment from the point of view of the Christian faith, it is clear both practically and theologically that nothing but the kingdom of God is good enough for a total, unified and shared peace or safe enough for such peace. Only the breadth and the openness of the love of God would provide space enough for a fulfilled human freedom. Therefore it is pretty clear that there are no prospects for peace in a positive, complete and humanly satisfactory or adequate sense. It is equally clear that a striving in the direction of a hoped for and longed for peace is a necessary and vital component in keeping human society open and alive. Problems about peace are not sufficient grounds for cynicism about peace or for concluding that peace must not be sought or considered. It is also necessary to note that because of the complications to which I am briefly referring, striving for peace is often, in practice, highly conflictual.

We are necessarily concerned, therefore, with the avoidance of war and the containing of conflict, and that in a world where conflict is endemic. This is where we confront the terrible urgency of our predicament. This is produced by the convergence of two things. The first is the escalation of nuclear weaponry and the second is the ideological polarization of conflict. This latter aspect of things is briefly pointed to by the dreadful caricature remark 'better dead than red'. There can rarely have been a more faithless remark than that. Clearly those who say it have no faith whatever in themselves, let alone in God. However, we will return later to this matter of ideology and seeing everything in over-sharp terms of one simple conflict. I want to proceed by considering the escalation of nuclear weaponry which so far has defied every attempt to slow it down. We seem to be faced with the implacable fact that the mere possession of nuclear weapons brings inexorable pressures to bear for their refinement and escalation. Here there is a terrible clarity which must never be obscured or forgotten or ignored, whatever are the practical complexities which follow on when we ask about what should be done. The terrible clarity is simply this. First we have far more than the means required to destroy ourselves in a matter of minutes. Secondly, if these means are used, they will destroy life and civilization in at least the northern hemisphere and threaten the whole planet. Thirdly, these means are set up for use. This, surely, is simple, clear and undeniable – even if it is barely sayable and barely thinkable – yet it is the simple position, so it is simply sayable and simply thinkable.

Nothing must be allowed to obscure this. Hence the very great importance of all movements and pressure groups designed to keep this simple fact and terrible clarity before the public and to press them on the politicians. This is the significance of CND peace movements and demonstrations like those of the women of Greenham. In the light of this terrible clarity we can also surely see the importance of all such demonstrations, including controlled and symbolic law-breaking by the law-abiding and those who seek a wider and more humane law. We have reached the limits of human possibility and the threat of human destruction, so that we are testing the very limits of human existence. It would therefore seem to be right in principle, in a responsible, restrained and organized way, to test the limits of civil disobedience and civil obedience. The principle would seem to be clear, although this does not settle the rights and wrongs of any particular demonstration or action. From a Christian point of view, I am clear that we have to face the well-established principle that there are occasions, rarer I am sure than many agitated activists think but more frequent than the more respectable will allow, when obedience to seeking the City of God requires disobedience to and in the cities of men.

A probable area of disobedience would be to refuse to have anything to do with nuclear civil defence. (For the sake of clarity I had better say that I am talking about civil defence concerned with responses to nuclear war. I am not arguing against the establishment of a nuclear emergency service concerned to deal with possible incidents in the field of the civil use of nuclear power. I myself see a clear distinction between issues of nuclear war and issues to do with the peaceful use of nuclear power. I am, of course, aware that not everybody agrees with this distinction, but the overwhelming importance

121

of the issues confronting us does not justify the blurring of important distinctions. I would argue and urge quite the contrary. Because the issues are so urgent, it is more than necessary, behind the front lines of urgent action, that we think hard, discriminate hard and act responsibly.)

I believe that nuclear civil defence should probably be rejected because the very idea of it obscures the terrible clarity of which I have been speaking. Nobody anywhere in our society, least of all in governmental or official circles, ought to do anything which lends credence to the notion that nuclear war is a possibility which can in any way be planned for or through which there is after all a reasonable chance of survival. Nuclear war can properly and humanly only be planned against as far as the civil government and the life of civilians are concerned. Of course, until we can effectively disarm it does have to be planned for by the military.

In the light of this terrible clarity about the real, actual and prepared total destructiveness of nuclear weapons systems, it is equally clear that arguments about the morality or immorality of possessing and planning to use nuclear weapons are neither here nor there. The nuclear weapons build-up is obscene, immoral and must be run down as soon as possible. The obscenity is heightened, if that is possible, by the absolutely monstrous waste of resources they represent in the face of the immense human and social needs that confront us in the Third World, in our inner cities, in our unemployed, in the needs of health and education and so on.

In the face of such a monstrous diversion of resources and the evident fact that we seem trapped in planning for our destruction at the cost of failure to use our immense resources for our urgent improvement, it might well seem that we deserve to destroy ourselves. But such feelings must be totally rejected. First, they could easily strengthen that strange but dangerously possible mixture of death-wish, fascination and apathy which

122

encourages people at least to live with and, quite possibly, to love the Bomb. Secondly, any such fatalism is contrary to any biblical and Christian understanding. The judgment of God is always so that men and women 'may repent and be saved', that is, the purpose of exposing sin and of showing up its utter destructiveness is so that people may repent, think new thoughts, see new ways forward and begin to do and receive new things which turn people from being on the way to death to being on the way to life.

Thus we must see the terrible threat we are under and the stark clarity with which it stands out as an opportunity and an invitation. But how should we respond to this opportunity and challenge? How can we best promote, if not the prospects for peace, at least the prospects for the avoidance of war and thus for keeping the way open to struggling hopefully and creatively with our various conflicts? Here the urgent clarity of the threat is not matched by the urgent clarity of a simple or a single answer. For the problem is: first, to prevent war breaking out; secondly, to find ways of running down nuclear armouries so that there is a general feeling and understanding that they are under control and the level of the threat can be steadily reduced; and then thirdly, to divert resources to peaceful and creative ends. All this is, inevitably, a large and complicated process of processes. Whether we understand the present position between the superpowers as a balance of terror which is for the time being to be maintained because it is the best deterrent we have or as the terror of balance out of which we must get as soon as possible, we are obliged to take into account the precariousness of the situation. So we have to weigh up the likely political and strategic effects of significant actions like unilateral nuclear disarmament or the rejection of the option of the first use of nuclear weapons under present circumstances and not under some moral ideal.

This cautious, temporizing and highly politically relativized remark may sound absurd and bitterly disappointing after what I have said about the terrible clarity of the threat which faces us and the clear obscenity and immorality of nuclear weapons. But this is where we have to face, and answer for ourselves, the basic and disturbing question about the nature of the world we live in and the nature of the God, if any, that we believe in and try to worship. I believe in God. I further believe that the God I believe in is the God pointed to by the basic pattern and promises of the Bible, the God who embodied himself as one of us in Jesus. I do not find any sufficient evidence in the Bible or in subsequent history which encourages me to believe that God is a large-scale worker of moral miracles whereby the stuff and struggles of our lives are rapidly and easily transformed into simple goodness and enjoyable peace. From the time of the first great prophets of Israel onwards at least, it has been plain that religious and moral demands on their own have never been sufficient to turn a society or group of any size from developing destructive ways to pursuing constructive ones. Repentance is an insight and an offering of the few which they have to contribute to the whole struggle. The redirection and replanning of the many in a society, or of the whole of a society, comes about through a bewildering and inextricable mixture of some creative moral and religious insights with the pressures of prudential self-interest, fear and force. We have no grounds therefore for expecting (still less relying on) miracles of conversion and transformation brought about by some single great gesture or one item of policy. We must hope and work for miracles of patience, survival and the creation of yet one more chance.

This must involve the urgent continuing of superpower negotiations for multilateral or bilateral disarmament. Whoever might go in for nuclear disarmament or declare themselves 'a nuclear-free zone', we are all in this one world and all under the aegis or the threat of what the USA and the USSR do, and we cannot opt out by a simple declaration of intent. Here we come back to the dangers of the ideological polarization of conflict to which I have earlier referred. We must do all in our power to make it clear that the conflict between the USA and the USSR is an ordinary imperial conflict and not the final conflict betwen good and evil, ideologically conceived. The absolutizing of this conflict is itself a devastating evil and perhaps the greatest obstacle to survival and therefore to opportunities for promoting peace. In my way of understanding things it is a particularly threatening form of practical atheism. For both sides identify their systems and their approaches to the world as absolute and to be maintained without compromise. Under God and, I would argue, under any reasonably humane view of the world and our prospects in it, all would be relativized. It would become clear, and I believe that it is clear, that there is no 'right way' either of being a human community or state or of working towards the easing of the death threat we live under.

That is to say that there is no ideal way which guarantees the achievement of properly desirable ends nor a way which can be justified as 'righteous' (whether by canons of communism, capitalism, Christianity, Islam, scientific humanism, pacifism, or what you will). Everything must be potentially negotiable and flexible. At the same time, however, we must maintain a proper respect for and a proper loyalty to our commitments, visions and hopes. The necessity to negotiate and compromise in no way undermines the imperative to maintain long-term commitments to the increase of opportunities for freedom, justice and welfare. On the other hand we must not be too sure that 'our' way of seeing things and doing things is necessarily in all aspects better than 'theirs' or that 'they' have no case. This does not involve any simple-minded trust. There is no realistic way forward which permits us to ignore the realities and inevitabilities of conflict, at both the pragmatic and moral levels.

Empires have always contended for power and influence, whatever ideological excuses or interpretations have been offered. There are also real and deep conflicts over what is involved in the 'good life' and there are serious grounds for abhorrence of what is done in the name of communism. Whatever criticisms are necessarily to be made against ourselves, the situation is not indifferent. It is quite clear that communism breeds totalitarianism and that totalitarianism is an evil to be resisted. So romantic acts of trust are no substitute for resoluteness in practicable self-defence. Unrealistic trust is not a useful political virtue. But distrust must not be allowed to dominate political judgment.

Today it is literally 'vital' (a matter of life and death) to be able to appreciate the point of view of those whom we have real reasons both to distrust and to resist. Our opponents have a serious point of view. It is really held. It has much to be said for at least some of it. And they are clearly seriously threatened. Like us they are human beings trapped in a deeply threatening world. It is one world and we have all contributed to its threatening nature by various versions of idealism, sin and indifference. So for the sake of survival and peace we need to be set free from turning possibly dangerous and to some extent evil human beings into malignant and all-powerful demons. Just as we should prevent ourselves seeing our own side as righteous angels of light. The task is to survive together so that we live together and out of this living together to look for ways forward. We have to face up to the simple threat of death with its terrible clarity and in the light of this to negotiate our way through the complexities of life.

Some of the practical considerations which arise from the arguments outlined above include the following. First, there is no sufficient case for Britain's retaining 'an independent deterrent'. It obscures our actual and total dependence on the wider US and NATO alliances. The case for having our own deterrent looks like a false and dangerous fantasy produced by that sort of independence and aggressive nationalism which is precisely one of the main contributors to the threat of death which faces us all. Arguments about and efforts for maintaining our deterrent distract attention from our main and vital concern for policies of survival and then reconciliation. And the waste of resources in the face of our local as well as global poverty is monstrous. Secondly, we have nevertheless to retain our membership of NATO and the process of giving up our own deterrent must be part of negotiations within that alliance. There can be no substitute for continuing, uncertain and compromising negotiation. There is no magical, miraculous stroke which will, overnight, multiply the chances of peace. Peace is a possibility derived from costly, hopeful and faithful persistence deriving from a realistic awareness both of the threats and the possibilities.

Thirdly, everyone must be constantly reminded that the two over-riding pressures upon us are the threat of death and the necessity of having to live together. The over-riding aim of arms negotiations therefore is the prevention of war, not the prevention of victory by the other side or the achievement of victory by our own. The immediate prize to be aimed at is survival and the opportunity to live together in the hope of better things. This means, for example, that negotiations about arms limitations must be based on *quid pro quos* about arms restrictions and inspections. Extraneous demands concerning such matters as human rights or withdrawal of influence from this country or that are not part of negotiating improvements in our chances of survival. They are separate matters to pursue as we survive.

Fourthly, on a broader front, more and more attention should be concentrated on the issues of economy and poverty. The relativizing of our ideologies under the threat of death ought to help us to see that we do not have a crisis of capitalism with a saving communism waiting in the wings or vice versa. We have a total industrial and economic crisis, with the communist countries sharing in the crisis of production, and all of us are without the means or the will to organize ourselves to share resources effectively in a way which will also multiply resources and at the same time protect the earth.

A principal prudential reason therefore for negotiating arms reduction and mutual systems of control is the crippling burden of cost. Neither the US nor Russia can much longer afford the consumption of such huge resources and nor can the rest of us. This is one more way in which pressures of self-interest and fear could come together with such moral insights and hope as we can muster to move us in a creative and morally desirable direction.

Finally, and for the same reason, we must encourage continuing work with enthusiasm on all possible fronts and not become single-issue dominated. The fear of death must not become panic and hysteria in the face of which the threat or tensions will be further heightened and possibilities of negotiation and manoeuvre be further limited. Every negotiation, pressure group or campaign for wider welfare, justice or freedom is a worthwhile contribution to the human struggle for sufficient peace to enable survival, growth and search. As the Bomb makes it clear that we must live together, it may also free us to find better and more just ways of living together. Thus our last chance may still be our best chance.

At any rate we must not believe that all is yet lost. Only when we so believe will it be lost ... Until then we have every reason to pursue the prospects of peace. First, by doing all we can to remind everyone, and especially the politicians, of the stark reality and the immediate urgency of the nuclear threat. Secondly, by insisting that negotiations must be unremitting and totally serious. The aim and the end of such negotiations is survival and not victory. If and as we survive then we can strive for the values we seek and over which we shall remain in conflict. And finally we contribute to the prospects of peace by keeping our own faith and hope alive. Hopelessness is certain death. Faith and struggle and reflection can always offer us a chance of life and the keeping open of further prospects for peace.

10

How Green is our Future?

'How green is our future?' The plain and simple answer to that question is that unless our future *is* green then we have no future. We are not talking about a fringe or a fad but about a question of survival and the source of either human destruction or human hope.

If we take a sober and matter-of-fact look into the future, then we are clearly faced with possibilities, indeed likelihoods, which are apocalyptic. Perhaps the most threatening of all the current trends and tendencies which severally and collectively combined call our future in question is that tendency of the presently prosperous and the currently powerful to defend their temporary prosperity and their uncertain power by dismissing the presentation of facts about what is happening to the world and to the majority of the inhabitants of it as the peddling of gloom and doom by persons who specialize in negativity. Perhaps this has always been the case. People who attempt to take long-term and more widely human views have great difficulty in getting what they see across to those who are currently doing well – and who therefore tend to disregard the evidence that there is not much future in their particular form of doing well and that, also, very much of the human race is actually doing badly, not least because of their ways of doing well.

The contradiction in our present ways of doing well is clearly brought out if we take a look at ourselves in the shadow of – or perhaps in the light of – all the turbulance and decline in the financial markets of the world in the past two weeks or so. Whatever else may be properly deduced from this turmoil and instability, one thing seems to be clear. We are living beyond our means. The central symptom of this which, as far as I can see, is taken by all commentators to be at the heart of the shake-up, is the American budget deficit and trading deficit. The richest country in the world is living so far beyond its income that other countries or speculators are no longer prepared to invest any more in its future capacity to earn and expand further. But here we come to something which leads into the questions of a Green future. We are also in the paradoxical situation that even though, in terms of the global system which affects us all, 'we' are living beyond our means, there are immense numbers of people, a majority in the Third World and a substantial minority in the First World, who do not command the means to live. In the Third World this is expressed in the millions of people who can scarcely subsist, let alone exist. In the First World the problem is expressed in the comparative poverty of a substantial number of people who are often grouped together in particular areas and the tendency for the worse off to become worse off. So we are living beyond our means and very many people do not have the means to live anything like a human life as enjoyed by those who, at the moment, live off living beyond their means. An acute symptom of this paradox is the Third World debt crisis wherein some poor countries have to depress the standard of living of their inhabitants who are already living very close to any subsistence standard in order to pay the interest on money which they have to borrow in order to pay the interest on the debt they already have. Clearly this cannot go on; something must give. But what must give? And what are the means we are living beyond?

Here we are brought to the wider and deeper implications for any viable, human and global future of the recent loss of confidence and computerized hiccough in the financial markets of the world. Clearly, if we are living beyond our means then we cannot expect to spend our way out of our problems. But the philosophy (if it can be dignified by that name) of the markets and producers who at present dominate the world seems to be that we can – if we can produce enough *growth* to extend and support further spending power. Here two very practical, extremely sharp and potentially apocalyptic questions arise. First, can the world stand that sort of growth to anything like the extent needed or assumed? (And this quite apart from the question of whether the dog-eats-dog system of competition would be stable enough to produce such growth anyway.) Secondly, what does this way of dealing with our problems do to the poor – who are still very much in the majority in our world – and can the countries of the world stand the stresses and strains of that – almost regardless of whether the effects on the poor are morally and humanly tolerable? With regard to the reliance on growth as such we have to face the horrendous realities of ecological erosion. With regard to the effects of this sort of growth, sought after by our current market system and our current financial arrangements, we have to face the shame-making and prudentially threatening realities of what I have come to call 'the barbed wire divide'.

As to ecological erosion, we all know really, and we all know clearly, that we are steadily using up the non-renewable resources and even the very substance of our strictly limited and heavily populated planet at rates which are debatable with regard to each particular resource but in an overall way which is undeniable. Forests are being felled without restraint, despite repeated warnings, and this not only destroys the possibility of a steady growth of further trees but encourages atmospheric changes which lead to deserts, which are also encouraged by the erosion of soil when the trees have gone. The ozone layer which helps make sunlight healthy and life-giving when it reaches us is under threat from our pollution and as good as pierced already in some recognizable spots. The disappearance of living species proceeds apace and the en-couraging and multiplying efforts of conservation are at the same time further symptoms of how we are turning the world into a desert. A small but significant symptom of our problem is experienced by anyone who is a keen walker in what used to be remote country places. So many people traverse the Pennine Way or climb Snowdon or walk in the Dove Valley that the paths are worn away, strips around the recognized routes become deserts and more and more efforts are needed to shore up a path and keep it fit for walking on. It is great that so many people have both the leisure and the longing to enjoy the countryside. But the fact remains that we are literally wearing it out. This is both a symptom and a parable of what we are doing to all the resources and beauties and liveliness of the earth.

Along with this goes the threatening social symptom of the barbed-wire divide. This symbol came into my head and has stayed hauntingly with me ever since I happened to see a short sequence on television news which showed Archbishop Runcie visiting Soweto with Archbishop Tutu. One sequence was filmed, so to speak, from outside in, and running across the centre of the screen was a barbed-wire entanglement – to mark, as it seemed to me, the need to defend white prosperity from black poverty. About the same time I also saw a brief moment of a film about the United States' Mexican border and the need for ceaseless vigilance and pretty violent measures to protect that border against the steady flow of poor people from the South pressing into a dreamt-of Eldorado in the United States – and incidentally running, some of them, drugs and other illegalities. The film implied that nothing would actually keep the tide back. Again I had the sense of the have-nots pressing desperately, although as yet not with any organized violence, into the land of the haves – where they would, of course, find many fellow have-nots. For the 'barbed-wire divide' is symbolic also of increasing divisions in both this country and the United States. We may here mis-call it the North-South divide and so kid ourselves that it does not really exist by an over-literal appeal to the term, the selective use of statistics and protests about the amount of public money that has been put into named areas. But the reality of the clear – and worsening – division between those who are in the system and can increasingly purchase its benefits, and those who are out of the system and who can never get the chance of either forming a market or joining in a market, is evident and undeniable. Will it be necessary to hive them all off into ghettos, surrounded by barbed wire, and patrolled, I suppose, by increasing numbers of police, and probably, soldiers?

This, I think, is not a party political question but a fundamental human and survival question, pressed upon each one of us by whatever it is that gives us a particular concern and longing for a sustainable and prospering human future. And what focusses all this on the question of a *Green* future is that, at the moment, what organized political and industrial hopes and procedures there are for the future of the world and the prosperity of each one of us are quite literally invested in growth – that is, in growth in consumption financed by purchasing power, which purchasing power is cash produced from increasing growth and increasing consumption. Clearly it cannot work from strictly factual and physical reasons and clearly it ought not to work because of the destruction of our glorious earth and of the miseries of human beings which it inflicts. It almost seems unnecessary to add to the apocalyptic pressures by bringing in the threats of nuclear war and the uncertainties of nuclear power, but they must clearly never be

134

forgotten. It may be that these threats are at last being seriously reduced and it may be that nuclear power can be handled in sufficiently positive and safe ways, but to do either of these things successfully requires great trust, great patience and great collaboration. Shall we get this in a world made so unstable and uncertain by ecological erosion, the barbed wire divide and global financial instability?

I want to end by outlining my reasons for holding that while the pressures which demand green responses threaten us with apocalypse and warn us of our last chance, they can and should be responded to as our best chance. I shall outline this in Christian and biblical terms because my understanding of, and commitment to, the ultimate, vibrant and hopeful reality of the universe takes the form of faith in God through Jesus Christ. As I am convinced that Jesus is a central and decisive way into the truth and passion of the God who is overall, in all and for all, I expect other human believers and seekers to be able to resonate with, and pick up from, what I have to say, even if they would not believe, or articulate, their ultimate commitments and hopes in my Christian way.

I believe that the apocalyptic pressures upon us can and should be read and responded to as the pressures of the judgment of God. We are collectively and comprehensively failing in the love of our neighbour. We are blasphemously, conceitedly and indifferently failing in our stewardship of the earth and we are worshipping and giving ourselves up to greed, consumption and sensuality. These are the perennial simple and basic sins against the great commandments. 'You shall love the Lord your God with all your heart, with all your strength, with all your mind and with all your soul . . . and your neighbour as yourself.' These are the conditions for prosperous and fruitful living together. Greed, consumption and seeking more and more are simply idolatry of ourselves and once you put yourself and its indulgences into the centre you get not a god but a devil, and all the good things of selves which are open to God and related to neighbours are lost. (For example both enterprise and technology which could be goods used for all become gods which threaten to destroy all.) The earth is offered to us as a gift, a promise and a shared good. But if riches increase and we set our hearts upon them, we despoil, destroy and cut off our own best future. And, as the famous parable of the Good Samaritan so devastatingly points out, the question always is 'and who *is* my neighbour?' The purely factual answer now is: 'everyone on the globe'. So getting love of the neighbour and stewardship of the globe properly lined up on the love, the creativity and the worship of God becomes a more and more pressing practical necessity.

But this takes some learning and even more responding to. Hence we move towards apocalyptic destruction by eroding the earth, increasing the poor, divorcing cash-making from wealth-producing and providing weapons and technologies which can destroy us. Clearly unless we repent – that is, re-think, replan, reorganize and realign – we shall all perish. What chance is there of this repentance actually happening? Every chance, for there is God and we do remain in his image and can resonate, respond and renew. The God of the Bible who is the God and Father of our Lord Jesus Christ is clearly a God of judgment and wrath who exercises that judgment and wrath to save men and women in his image and to further his loving but risky purposes of creation and fulfilment. Therefore sharp destructive pressures are not occasions for either cowardly avoidance or panic-filled confusion but precisely opportunities for discovering resources we did not think we had for new thoughts, new directions, new efforts and new social, in-dustrial, economic and political constructions. God stands for a possibility of newness which is, as yet, beyond our conceiving or our dreaming. 'Except you repent you will all perish.' But that means you can repent and you need not perish.

So we must not fear to raise, to press and to pursue the presently unanswerable questions if these questions are real and if they are urgent. The 'green' agenda is clearly real and clearly urgent. We must find ways of moving over from greedy, ever-increasing consumption by the well-off to sharing and suitable consuming by everyone. We must find ways of breaking up global markets and dominating multinational companies which do not and cannot care for either local viability or global sustainability into regional markets, localized trading and organized contributions of self-help and mutual exchanges based much more on new forms of barter than old forms of exploitation. We must plan about, agree about and enforce regional and global programmes of conservation and defence against all-embracing pollution and all-devouring resource-use. We have to realize that we are one world and must get beyond being dominated by competition and conflict into forms of negotiation, collaboration and the production, preservation and circulation of common wealth for common aims that are sufficiently just to be acceptable and sufficiently controlled to be sustainable.

All this may sound like pie in the sky and it is certainly liable to the apparently practical and down-to-earth objection: but what shall we do now and who will do it? But to this the reply must again and again be that unless we discover how to change we have no future which is anything but nasty, brutish and short. A creative and sustainable future lies through finding ways together of perceiving and facing unanswerable questions until the answers appear or we discover that we need ask and respond to different questions. There is no future in the twenty-first century based on nineteenth-century nostalgias about either Market powers or workers' powers. To refuse to acknowledge and to face the questions is not to be practical but to be promoting a fools' paradise which will become more and more an idiots' hell.

Moreover answers, or the beginnings of answers, are appearing and there are already a vast network of so far small and uninfluential groups throughout the world which are wrestling with these things. Some of the E. F. Schumacher's suggestions are very down-to-earth and perfectly practicable – once there is sufficient political will. It is great stupidity and totally unhistorical to suppose that we must go on as the economics developed over the last two hundred years appear to require. (Although *what* economics? We always need to remember that for economists the real world is a special case. I suspect that what hinders us is economic myths and folklore, and not economic science and analysis.) Nothing but our own obtuseness and self-serving ignorance requires us to insist on going on as we are and heading for destruction.

So the green agenda must be pressed, and green reflections, experimentations and analysis must be pursued. Alternatives there can be and alternatives there will be. First, all who are alerted to the facts must press the centrality of the issues and resist all attempts at diversions by those who press what they call immediate practicality in order to evade the present threats of future fatuity. Secondly, more and more people should be ready to use the skills they have learned from all the disciplines of the modern world to dream up, work out and work at alternatives in the direction of shared and sustainable food resources, local and regional economics, alternatives to a money market and a cash nexus which has taken off from all reasonable wealth-creating realities and so on. Thirdly, we have to stress the hopefulness of the pressures which are upon us. For instance, given our technological and biological know-how there is no real problem about feeding everyone in the world to a level which sets them free for a reasonably human life and to make their contribution to a viable and enjoyable society. It can be done. It is just that as yet we do not know how to organize it and will not put our energies into finding out. But now the threats of apocalypse make it clear that we must once again dream for a better and more human future for all and that this is what we must work for. Otherwise none of us will have a world.

So I end by daring to express the faith and the hope that God still knows what he is doing. If we can get a sufficient minority of people to see sufficiently how nuclear control, ecological conservation, and juster and more shared ways of producing, distributing and consuming are our last chance, then the pressures will become our best chance and all the gifts of human science, technology, enterprise, inventiveness, altruism and good will can be redirected to building a better world for all – a world with a future and a world which continues to offer all its riches, wonder and mystery to us, our children and our children's children, while we all press on with the mystery and the glory of the pilgrimage which is offered to us. Except we repent we shall all perish. But if we use our immense powers and skills and imaginations for repentance, what a future lies before us!